FAITH
FLOWS
DOWN

Watershed Family Resources

Faith Flows Down
Copyright © 2015 Watershed Family Resources

Requests for information can be made at www.watershedfamilies.com

For Noël, my partner in life and in the home.

And, for Roe, Abram, Sophie, and Lottie.
I pray for faith to flow down through you to
1000 generations.

Acknowledgements

Over the last thirteen years of ministering to children and families I've been sharpened and refined by many great champions of ministry. This book is the fruit of countless clarifying conversations over the years that challenged me to think, research, and study the Word. I could never thank every one of my influencers, but I'm so grateful for all those God used in my life to form my beliefs and practices for family ministry.

Thank you to my read team: Russ Barksdale, Marty Collier, Scott Oldenburgh, Jeff Kirkpatrick, Mark Williams, Cody Donald, Emily Greetham, and Lauren Sudberry. Each of you are incredibly busy and I cherish your gift of time and input to make this book better.

I also want to take a moment to recognize the incredible family ministry team I get to work with every single day: Lauren Van Hoy, Janeene Morrison, Misty Nailon, Michelle King, Stephen Rickels, John Simmons, Bradley Barksdale, and Karen Rajendran. I'm honored to build the kingdom with such great partners and friends.

Steve Parten, Darren Miley, Melissa May, Jennifer Van Norman, Ryan Vaughn, and Brad McNair were also instrumental in the formation of the principles found in Faith Flows Down. You all have had a positive impact on my ministry life.

Finally, thank you Noël. You are my greatest encourager and I absolutely love leading a family with you.

TABLE OF CONTENTS

FOREWORD

I was a much better parent before I had kids.

When my wife Noël and I were just beginning our marriage we joined a young married Sunday school class at our church. As it happens, the couples in that class played fast and loose with the definition of "young," and we found ourselves in weekly Bible study with many members who were much older and further advanced in life experience. Every week they talked about their problems and frustrations in raising children. As a class we listened with empathy, offered biblical advice, and prayed with passion for God to bring peace and wisdom into these homes.

Well, that's what everyone else did. Not me. I sat silently and judged these inferior parents in my mind.

On the drive home from church I would smugly explain to Noël exactly what these parents should do, and how I would do everything differently when we had children. Everything better.

And then we had a kid.

And another one.
Then two more after that.

One day I need to drive back to that town and apologize to every parent from my old Sunday school class. Parenting is tough stuff. Many days you feel like you're walking through a mist of uncertainty on a path you've never walked before. The parents I knew back then were valiantly trudging ahead through the parental haze the best they knew how. Contrary to what my younger self believed, there are no easy answers in raising children. Those who are willing to roll up their sleeves and do the hard work of teaching, correcting, challenging, praying, and intentionally leading their kids are now my heroes.

At one time I was quite the expert. Now I'm a dad who struggles at times to know what to say. Sometimes I'm not as present in the moment as I need to be. Sometimes I lose my temper and embarrass myself in front of my wife and children. Before kids I truly thought I had all the answers, but having real living and breathing small humans in my home has humbled me and taught me some tough lessons. Here are a few:

- Every one of my children is different. Just because something works with one, doesn't mean it will work with another.
- Kids are sinful from birth. The sin nature that lives in me is alive and well in them too.
- Just when you get in a groove with raising a child, their developmental stage will change and you've got to figure them out all over again.
- I am much more selfish than I thought before kids came along and shined a spotlight on what I choose to do with my time, leisure, and resources.

These lessons go down like giant horse pills, and it seems I have to keep swallowing them over and over again. Thankfully I benefit from two things: A gracious, PATIENT Savior, and a family who loves me and extends more forgiveness than I deserve. It is only through His power and their support that I can lead my home effectively for God's glory.

For quite a few years I worked as a pastor to children. I didn't start out wanting to serve children full-time. In fact, I took my first children's ministry position only because I was working in a print shop, bored out of my mind, and badly wanting to work in a church. I secretly thought, *"I'll just do this job for a little while until something better comes along."* I knew enough to understand if I spoke that thought out loud the church would never hire me, so I said all the right things and got the job. But here is where the unexpected happened (Don't you love when God does unexpected things?). In a short time in that position I became very passionate about seeing kids introduced to God's truth, experience salvation in Jesus, and grow into disciples who live on mission with God. Children's ministry took hold of my heart and still hasn't let go.

It didn't take long serving kids in church for me to understand just how valuable parents are in the spiritual formation of children. If I didn't see it myself, I got the message from every children's ministry book I read, class I took, and conference I attended. Engaging parents into the work of spiritual leadership has been the national ministry conversation for more than a decade and it continues today. But even if no one was talking about the importance of parents, it was easy to see as a young minister in my first church. I learned quickly how little of my teaching children retained from Sunday to Sunday. I saw how easily kids got confused by the deeper matters of faith such as salvation and baptism without a loved one walking alongside to help navigate. I witnessed for myself how kids from homes with spiritually engaged parents were so much better prepared for biblical discussion. I learned that faith flows down.

Over time my passion to serve kids turned into a passion to help parents lead kids.

Today I'm a family pastor. With all my heart I want to see homes become the primary place to foster spiritual growth... it's just more effective that way. Don't get me wrong, I am fully aware that our churches are full of people who found faith without strong spiritual leadership from their parents. God is big enough and good enough to work that way too. However, to give our kids the best opportunity to become champions for Jesus, parents need to break that cycle and rise up to lead, teach, equip, and encourage.

Right at the start I want to tell you that reading this book reveals the right spirit in you. No one picks up a book about influencing children for Jesus just to pass the time. There are a lot of things you could devote your energy to, but this subject matters more than any other. It matters now and it matters for generations to come. Right this very second you are creating a legacy of faith that you will pass along to your children and grandchildren, whether you have kids in your house right now or not. The things you believe, the things you put into practice, the faith you display, and the stories you live right now will create a foundation for those who come behind you.

So way to go! I'm so glad you've decided to spend this time with me, exploring the subject of passing faith down to children. Our conversation will be in three parts. In part one we'll discuss why and how we spiritually develop our sons and daughters at home by seizing opportunities, creating opportunities, and leveraging special opportunities for family faith talks. In this section I can't wait to tell you what Deuteronomy 6 tells us about leading our homes and hopefully encourage you to believe you really can do this thing called spiritual leadership. In part two we will investigate faith in children: what they need to know, how their faith is different than yours, and what conversations you need to have to prepare them for God's call of salvation. Finally, in part three we will look at the family of faith. What are some practices families participate in together to honor God? How do parents prepare now so that they leave behind a legacy of faith for children and grandchildren in the future? Hopefully we will answer these questions together.

At the beginning of this book you are probably thinking one of three things:

1. If you are thinking, "Yes! I am ready to begin and find out all that I can do from morning to night to be the best parent the world has ever known," to you I say… Thanks for reading this book! There's a good chance you're either a brand new parent or longing for the day when you raise a child in your home. One day I'm sure you'll be a great mom or dad, just please don't judge me when I seek support for my parenting mistakes in small group.

2. If you are thinking, "Great. Someone has recommended me read yet another book that will make me feel awful about missed opportunities, busy schedules, and parental shortcomings," to you I say… I promise I won't. In fact, this book might be the breath of fresh air you need to give yourself grace and get moving down the road to real home discipleship. Hang with me for a few chapters and give me a chance.

3. If you are thinking, "I know spiritually leading my kids is important, but I have no idea how to do it," to you I say… I've been there and I understand. You may be closer to answers than you think. Turn to chapter one and we'll start the first step together.

PART ONE

LETTING
FAITH
FLOW
DOWN

1

RELAX AND LOVE GOD

First, a play entitled *The Perfect Family of Faith.*

As our scene begins Mother, Father, and their daughter Mabel are sitting around a kitchen table piled high with homemade dishes and fresh vegetables. Father is wearing a coat and tie, and his napkin (cloth of course) is folded neatly in his lap. Mother is dressed equally sharp in a linen dress she saves for special occasions. Mabel has already done all her homework and now waits patiently with her elbows as far as possible from the edge of the table. An upright piano sits in the corner. Suddenly Ricky, Mabel's older brother, runs into the kitchen slightly out of breath.

Ricky: I'm so sorry I'm late for family dinner and Bible study, father!

Father: I hope you have a good excuse, son. You know how important our family time with God is.

Ricky: Of course, dear father. I lost track of time helping box canned goods at the local food pantry. I just love serving the Lord and time simply got away from me.

Father: You are forgiven son. You've never given me a reason not to trust you before. Just try to be on time from now on.

Ricky: Yes sir.

Mabel: I know what you mean about serving, brother. I have the blessed opportunity to rake leaves tomorrow at the senior center and I'm not sure if I'll be able to sleep tonight from my excitement!

Ricky: Cool! And might I say that you are the best little sister a boy could ever want? I'm so thankful that you are in my family.

Mother: Alright you two... I know you could go on and on about how much you love each other, but now it's time to begin our devotional time.

Ricky and Mabel: (*together*) Yay!

Father: As you know, we've been working together to memorize the first four books of the New Testament. Dear, where did we leave off last week?

Mother: Luke.

Father: That's right... good old Luke. Tonight as we eat we will memorize another ten chapters together, but before we do I thought we'd have a little fun. On the way home from work I drove by the church and picked up a little surprise.

Mabel: Oh my goodness, what is it father?

Mother: Language Mabel.

Mabel: Sorry mother.

Father: My surprise is... hymnals!

Father reaches under the table and pulls out several hymnals with old, brown covers. The children gasp in surprise.

Ricky: Does this mean we get to sing together before dinner?

Father: Yes! As long as we can convince mother to accompany on the piano.
Mother: But dear, our food is getting cold.

Father: It is worth a little cold food for the chance to celebrate our great God in our own home.

Mother: Well, when you put it that way, how could I refuse? What would you like to sing first?

Mother stands and approaches the piano.

Mabel: Ooh… May I choose? My favorite song in the whole world is number 354.

As the family settles in to sing together the scene fades to black.

Does this sound like a night in your home? Please, please, please tell me the answer is no. If yes, we have a couple of issues right off the bat. First, you are probably not reading the right book… this one is not going to be very helpful to you. More importantly, there is a strong possibility that you have confused reality with the sitcoms you watched as a kid and may need some clinical help.

Of course this is not your family. This is no one's family. To even write a scene with a brother saying something nice to a sister is some sort of science fiction that would have to be set on a planet other than earth. Real family is messy and busy and overwhelming. Let's see if this sounds a little more accurate:

You were out late the night before watching a little league game go into extra innings, so today you wake up completely exhausted. Still, you drag yourself out of bed, leaving just enough time to pack lunches, sign homework sheets, brush teeth and hair, and get everyone buckled in the car. You screech through the school drop-off line way too fast, but the kids still arrive late to school by three minutes. After school, the pace picks up again. Dance class begins at 4:30pm and there's a birthday party across town immediately after that. You have barely enough time to drop off your child for tap class, swing through Target to buy a plastic piece of junk for a kid you've never met, and get back to the studio before your little dancer is dismissed from class. But then… crisis. You forgot to buy wrapping paper. You go back to the store for a gift bag and tissue paper (because who has time to wrap) and drop in the toy with minutes to spare before the party begins. Think… think… will your child get dinner at the party? The start time is 6:30pm, so probably not. A quick detour through a fast food place is required and then finally you are on your way. For two more hours you stand around awkwardly making small talk with other parents before finally going home. There you are greeted with the daunting task of getting a kid wired from birthday cake to settle down and do an hour's worth of homework. Late that night you don't even care there is icing dried in your child's hair, you just somehow miraculously get them still and under the covers. Exhausted again, you tumble into a heap on the couch and fall asleep in your clothes.

Is this a little closer to your reality? I thought so. If it's not little league, dance class, and birthday parties turning your days into chaos then it's probably something else. People are busy. Families are busy. And somewhere in all this bedlam parents are supposed to spiritually lead their children? How is that even thinkable?

I believe there are Christian, church-going parents all across our country who are convinced spiritual leadership is not possible… not for them anyway. They understand they are primarily responsible for teaching their kids the Bible, leading them to Jesus, and then helping them live abundant lives of faith; but they feel like utter failures in the endeavor. Many of us hear stories about families who are living on-mission for God together, enjoying meaningful times of prayer, or studying the Word together and it makes us feel terrible about our own scattered, frenetic lives. Many of us don't even try to fix the chaos of our days or insert spiritual activity into our schedule because we don't truly believe we are capable. Maybe you've tried to pray with your kids once and it felt painfully awkward, so you quit. Maybe you attempted to schedule a time for family devotionals, but after missing one or two weeks you gave up. You truly want your family to be like the faithful ones you hear about, but the spirit of defeat has overtaken you and you no longer trust yourself to lead. How did this happen?

Right from the start you must understand this incredibly important truth: your family has an enemy. Your enemy hates everything God loves… and God is a huge fan of family. Your Father placed you, your spouse, and your children together for the great goal of bringing glory to Him in the world. Your enemy wants to disrupt that plan.

Be serious! Be alert! Your adversary the Devil is prowling around like a roaring lion, looking for anyone he can devour. – 1 Peter 5:8 HCSB

The devil has a few weapons at his disposal to keep your home from being a place that fosters spiritual growth. The first two are obvious and fairly overt: sin and distraction. Both of these can do a lot of damage to families and must be taken seriously. Sin destroys relationships, creates discord in the home, and ruins closeness with God. Distractions like overloaded schedules and too much technology erode family life and teach children wrong priorities.

But I believe there is a third weapon Satan uses that cripples many good, well intending families. This scheme is so sly, so slick, that a lot of us don't even recognize it hanging around our necks like an anvil. We know when we are living in sin and we can feel when our lives are busy and without margin, but this weapon sneaks up and finds us unaware. I'm talking about **the spirit of defeat.**

THE SPIRIT OF DEFEAT

If sin knocks you down, the spirit of defeat keeps you there. Your enemy wants to keep you from taking up your God-given role as spiritual leader so that he can destroy your family. Make no mistake… that is his goal. Ever so slyly, he whispers lies that sound so much like the truth:

- You aren't good enough for your children.
- The church should handle this spiritual stuff. You don't know enough.
- Your kids know how you really are at home. They'll never accept biblical truth from you.
- You're just too busy.
- It's too late.
- You're the only family that can't make this work.

Do any of these sound familiar? The chances are really good at some point you've believed one of these lies or something similar from the pit of hell. Sure, we've all made mistakes as parents. We've probably spent seasons of busyness that taught wrong priorities to our children, and maybe we don't all have master's degrees in theology. But these lies are meant to take our short-comings and let them drive a wedge between where we are and where God wants to take us as leaders. Thankfully God extends grace to His followers so complete and so final that no wedge ever needs to exist, no matter what.

I love what the writer of Hebrews says about Jesus our great High Priest, who understands everything we go through in life:

Therefore, since we have a great high priest who has passed through the heavens—Jesus the Son of God—let us hold fast to the confession. For we do not have a high priest who is unable to sympathize with our weaknesses, but One who has been tested in every way as we are, yet without sin. Therefore let us approach the throne of grace with boldness, so that we may receive mercy and find grace to help us at the proper time. – Hebrews 4:14-16 HCSB

We boldly approach the throne of God based not on what we offer, but based purely and solely on the work of Jesus. There we find grace, mercy, and help to live life and lead our families in a God-honoring way. This grace doesn't run out. It doesn't dry up. It doesn't get used up. Grace and mercy pick us up off the floor and set us back on the narrow path.

Every. Single. Time.

We don't have to live with the spirit of defeat. If we try something and fail, we try again. If we drop the ball on teaching spiritual truth to our kids, we look up the answer in the Bible and give it another shot. If we make a mistake in front of our family, we admit our shortcoming and ask for forgiveness. Through Jesus, we can shut down the enemy when he tells us we are disqualified from leading our children spiritually. God's grace alone qualifies us for the job. Yes, we all need to continue to grow as disciples of Christ, but we don't have to wait until we are perfected to pass on our faith to our kids. News flash – that's not going to happen on this side of eternity. On your own you are not enough for your child. Through Jesus you absolutely can lead your home for the Glory of God.

"Through Jesus, we can shut down the enemy when he tells us we are disqualified from leading our children spiritually. God's grace alone qualifies us for the job."

And here's how you start:

REFRAME WHAT YOU BELIEVE
ABOUT SPIRITUAL LEADERSHIP

Think back to the little play that started this chapter. Ridiculous, right? Yet many of us believe something like this is the model of what home discipleship is supposed to look like, at least subconsciously. We believe that children are to sit still for extended periods of time, listen quietly to large passages of scripture, pray using big words that only preachers understand, and not mind a bit when parents ask them to turn off their video games.

That doesn't sound like the children I know.

At all.

Children are supposed to play and move and laugh and get a little silly. They don't learn and grow like adults because they are not adults! All of their energy, all of their playfulness, all of their crazy off-the-wall questions are part of God's design in kids. Why would we set up a model that works against the maturation process imprinted on children by the Perfect Creator? It doesn't make sense.

So let's rethink what we believe about home discipleship. Deuteronomy 6:4-9 is a foundational passage for casting vision for true family spiritual leadership.

> *Listen, Israel: The Lord our God, the Lord is One. Love the Lord your God with all your heart, with all your soul, and with all your strength. These words that I am giving you today are to be in your heart. Repeat them to your children. Talk about them when you sit in your house and when you walk along the road, when you lie down and when you get up. Bind them as a sign on your hand and let them be a symbol on your forehead. Write them on the doorposts of your house and on your gates.* [1]

This passage, called the Shema, is extremely important in Jewish culture. The Hebrew word "shema" means "hear" or "listen". It's the first word in this passage and a directive for the reader to pay attention because what follows is important. Followers of Judaism have quoted this passage twice daily for thousands of years. It's the first scripture Jewish children learn in their study of the Torah (the first five books of the Old Testament). In fact, Jesus quoted part of it to an expert of the law who asked, "Teacher, which command in the law is the greatest."

> *He said to him, "Love the Lord your God with all your heart, with all your soul, and with all your mind. This is the greatest and most important command. The second is like it: Love your neighbor as yourself. All the Law and the Prophets depend on these two commands."* – Matthew 22:37-40 HCSB

---

1   HCSB

At the center of everything is **loving God**. These verses tell us it's the single most important thing we can do. Learning to love the Father... really love Him... is where you start as a follower of Christ, and it's where you start as a parent too. Before anything else you fall deeply in love with God and His Word. You can't pass along something you don't have inside yourself.

My oldest son plays the trombone in his school marching band. I love to go hear him play at football games and eat things that are terrible for me. I'm that embarrassing dad who videos the trombone section during the *Mission Impossible* theme song with my phone. I have a blast being a band dad... but I'm no help at all. I've never played a brass instrument in my life. I don't know anything about slide positions, how to hold your lips, or how to clean out a spit valve. Do trombones have spit valves? See, I don't know anything. I'm going to have to ask my son tonight at home.

My wife Noël, on the other hand, knows a little bit about playing brass instruments. She played trumpet when she was in the school band, so she can help him run through scales and practice his technique at home. She has something to offer him because she's walked the path he's trying to walk now. All I can do is record video of the school's fight song while I munch on a Snickers bar.

You can't lead someone down a path you've never walked yourself. This is true of playing the trombone and it's true of spiritually leading your children. As a parent your first responsibility to your family is to love God with all of your heart, soul, and strength through His Son, Jesus. You foster this love affair by spending time in the Word and communing with God through meditation and prayer. It's not complicated... in fact, it's fundamental to every aspect of faith. Everything flows from a love relationship with God.

This is fantastic news! You don't need the latest, slickest approach to family discipleship. You don't need to be an expert in childhood education. You need to fall more in love with God and allow Him to change you, transform you, empower you... make you more for your family and for the kingdom. This is the absolute best thing for you, your children, and the people you influence. Here is my best advice for every parent who wants to raise children in a Godly way:

Relax.

Quit listening to the lies.

Fall more in love with God.

That's it. That's the starting point. From here faith flows down. If you are actively pursuing Christ daily, I can tell you that you are probably doing a better job of spiritually leading your kids than you think. It's a tired expression, but it's true… faith is more likely to be *caught* than *taught.* Your kids notice the mornings you spend reading the Bible. They watch when you take dinners to the homebound in your church. They see you choose honesty and integrity in the grocery store when the clerk gives you back too much change. You are modeling what it means to be a disciple of Christ and this is making an imprint on them you can't see right now. One day you will.

We'll talk about how to let your faith spill over to your children in the next chapter, but for now I'll say it again… **Relax**. Reframe everything you believe about leading your family. It doesn't have to be some ridiculous model that more closely resembles a stuffy adult Bible study. Free yourself from believing that you have to make your children sit still for an hour every day just so that you can do your job as spiritual leader. It's much more important who you ARE than what you DO.

So breathe in. Breathe out.

Love God. You're already halfway there.

Chapter Wrap Up

- Your family has an enemy with tools meant to stop you from spiritually leading your home: sin, distraction, and the spirit of defeat.

- Through Jesus we can overcome every feeling of inadequacy. His power and grace alone qualify us for the job of passing our faith down to our children.

- We need to reframe what we believe about home discipleship based on the teachings of Deuteronomy 6:4-9. Teaching God's Word doesn't have to be made up of stuffy, boring lessons. The Shema shows us a better way.

- The most important thing any parent can do to spiritually lead children is to fall in love with God and His Word.

Talk About It

The following are questions to answer yourself or talk about in a group.

1. What are some things you want to instill into your children as they grow? What do you want them to value or exhibit in their lives? Do you have a plan to develop these things?

2. Have you experienced the spirit of defeat in your own life? What effect did it have on you?

3. What lies from the enemy are you believing about yourself and your home?

4. How did you form your belief about what it means to spiritually lead a family? Have you been able to live up to your own ideals at home?

5. Are you actively pursuing a love relationship with God? What does it mean to you to fall deeply in love with your Heavenly Father so that it overflows into the lives of your family members?

2

LET IT OVERFLOW

Imagine a glass of water. The water in the glass represents everything inside of you that you want to pour into your children… all your hopes, dreams, and aspirations. You want to teach them to have great character and integrity. You want them to be kind to everyone, even those who are different and difficult to love. You want them to be responsible and have a good work ethic in school. Traits like these don't just happen, they take effort, work, and repetition. So you pour yourself out like a glass of water over your children and give them everything you have inside toward this end. The world will applaud your sacrificial parenting and surrender of all things for the sake of your child. Surely this is what good parenting is supposed to look like!

Actually there is something wrong with this picture. Really wrong.

If, in this illustration you are represented by the glass of water, you are left completely empty when your effort is spent. Worse, all you've poured out on your children has washed away or evaporated and they need more from you, but you have nothing left to give. You emptied every ounce of energy, wisdom, and patience you have stored inside, but the kids need more. What do you do now?

Have you ever felt empty as a parent? I have.

I have experienced the deep exhaustion of feeling completely spent and re-alizing more is required. It mostly happens for me these days when I come home from a long day only to discover math homework waiting for me. I hate math homework. We all asked the question growing up, "why do I need to know this stuff?" Now I know the answer… because thirty years later I have to recall it all and explain it to my frustrated children.

Some nights I sink into my chair after the kids go to sleep, zone out to some-thing mindless on TV, and check out. The next morning I wake up just as tired as when I went to bed. I'm not thinking about the big important lessons like integrity and character, I'm just making sure my son gets his homework turned in and somehow getting myself through the day without falling asleep at my desk. For these times I need something bigger, something stronger, and outside of myself to keep me focused on the stuff that really matters.

I need God.

This is where the wisdom of the Shema shines like the bright star and gives hope for parents. First we fall in love with God and His commands with all our heart, soul, and strength; then we let our relationship with God spill out onto our children.

Imagine again the glass of water. This time, mentally place the glass in a foun-tain that never runs dry. The glass fills to the brim and overflows with cool, refreshing water that pours down from us over our children in a never-ending waterfall. The glass never empties and there is more than enough for your entire family to stay submerged in the water of life.

> The one who believes in Me, as the Scripture has said, will have streams of living water flow from deep within him." John 7:38 HCSB

I love the wisdom of the Deuteronomy 6 style of parenting! Loving God first means spiritual leadership doesn't come at the expense of my own depletion. Also, my children don't have to rely on my strength and understanding to grow spiritually. They benefit from the "streams of living water" flowing out of me as I commune with God through the Word and prayer. This is truly a better way! Yes, I may still be tired at the end of the day, but the Spirit can still flow through me and empower me to love, guide, and serve my kids… even against dreaded obstacles like math homework.

Every day we have the opportunity to have faith talks in our home. Some opportunities come up naturally in the course of life, and others we can create and foster through spiritual activity. The key to rising up and seizing these opportunities is **intentionality.** We must intentionally look for ways to let what God is doing in us overflow to our children. I believe there are three methods to let faith flow down to our families: seized opportunities, created opportunities, and special opportunities. All three methods deserve a place in our plan to spiritually develop our kids, but the first two carry most of the heavy lifting, so let's start with those.

SEIZED OPPORTUNITIES

Look again at the way faith talks are described in Deuteronomy 6, this time focusing on the second half of the instructions found in verses 6-9:

> *These words that I am giving you today are to be in your heart. Repeat them to your children. Talk about them when you sit in your house and when you walk along the road, when you lie down and when you get up. Bind them as a sign on your hand and let them be a symbol on your forehead. Write them on the doorposts of your house and on your gates.*[2]

When Moses wrote these words he incorporated a grammatical device called a "merism". A merism is a term for using contrasting terms to communicate a totality. For instance, if I said, "I searched high and low for the remote, but I couldn't find it," what I mean is, "I looked everywhere I knew to look and now I'm tired of looking, so I'm going to make my children press the buttons on the TV while I sit in my chair." Moses' instructions to talk about the commands of God when you sit, when you walk, when you get up, and when you go to sleep really mean to do it everywhere and all the time.

The family ministry model described in Deuteronomy 6 is not a rigid, formalized version of home lessons. Rather it's an as you go, real life way of leading your children toward God and His truth. When the Spirit of God is filling your soul and spilling over, discipleship happens anywhere and at any time. This isn't a picture of some forced, faked dinner table Bible lesson. It's not describing some unattainable level of instruction that goes against the very spirit of a child. The Shema encourages the people of God to pass along our faith in the natural context of daily life. We talk about God's commands at home, in the street, in the morning, at night... in other words, wherever and whenever we possibly can. But for this to work we have to intentionally look for opportunities and anticipate God's work in our families.

God is orchestrating **divine appointments** every day in your home. These are moments in which the conditions and conversations in your family give you the opportunity to point toward God's truth. If you aren't actively walking in communion with God and drinking from the well of His wisdom, these appointments can be easily missed. But when we are engaged in God's activity in our home, ordinary days turn into training sessions for spiritual champions.

> "When we are engaged in God's activity in our home, ordinary days turn into training sessions for spiritual champions."

Let me show you what I mean... Say you walk into your young child's room today to find him coloring on the walls in permanent marker. He's created an elaborate portrait of your face on the body of a dragon. Oh, and he's drawn your face really fat. In this moment you can respond in several ways. One thing you can do is take all the markers from your child and put him in a "time out" chair facing the very wall he just defaced so that he can "think about what he's done." After several minutes you tell him to get up and come say he is sorry. All that's left now is for you to try to match the paint at the local hardware store the following Saturday (Was it ecru, cream, or off-white? And what in the world is the difference?).

If you are actively looking for teachable moments however, you can see this incident for what it is... a divine appointment to teach God's truth to your child's heart. Maybe you still use a time out chair, but in this case you don't just tell your child to say, "sorry." This time you sit him on your lap and tell him something like this:

"Hey buddy, you made a mistake, but I still love you. I'm always going to love you no matter what. You are more important to me than a wall, and you're important to God too. He loves you EVEN MORE than I do, and there's nothing you can do to change that. He knows everything about you... the good and the bad... and He is still CRAZY about you. Isn't that amazing?"

Every day we have a chance to speak truth and model discipleship in our home if we look for divine appointments. God will orchestrate opportunities to lead our children toward Him and His Word, but we have to stay watchful.

They can come in all sorts of situations:

- When your child comes home from school lonely because no one would sit with her on the bus, you can remind her God will never leave her or forsake her (Hebrews 13:5).

- When your child celebrates a soccer win you can tell him that every gift and talent comes from the Father to use for His glory (James 1:17).

- When your child is hurt by a friend you can comfort her by sharing that God is near to the brokenhearted (Psalm 34:18).

- When you catch your child teasing another child in the neighborhood you can correct him by explaining that Jesus commands His followers to love our neighbors as ourselves (Matthew 22:39).

When we first drink in God's truth and then let if overflow, we can seize opportunities like these to help kids see God's truth in every situation. Sometimes we like to compartmentalize our faith… act as though the Bible is for Sundays and morning devotions and the rest of the time is "real life." In reality, God's truth IS real life, and we show that to our children by intentionally infusing faith into every facet of our day, public and private. As parents, we have to act like we believe the Apostle Peter's writing in 2 Peter 1:3, "His divine power has given us everything required for life and godliness through the knowledge of Him who called us by His own glory and goodness."[3] Power through the knowledge of God for life and godliness… this is exactly what our kids need!

There are three disciplines we can practice daily to be ready to seize opportunities for spiritual leadership: **read the Word**, **meditate on the Word**, and **model the Word**. First, we have to actually spend time reading the scriptures on a consistent basis. There's no shortcut for this. No podcast, Christian book, or Sunday morning preaching can take the place of opening the Bible and exploring God's truth on our own. Have you ever been called upon in a group to give your thoughts on a book you haven't read? I have… it's awful. I've stumbled and faked my way through answers, all the while knowing quite clearly that I'm fooling exactly zero people. That's no way to approach arming yourself with God's Word daily. You don't want to fake or guess your way through, and you don't want to discover life-giving scriptures second-hand either. Sure, there's nothing wrong with a great book that helps you think

---

3   HCSB

through difficult concepts. There's also nothing wrong with a daily devotional on your phone or emailed to you with an inspirational thought. There are a thousand resources that can provide this type of service for you, but these things are not a replacement for the pure, unadulterated Word of God. You must go straight to the source to find your daily bread. That's the first step in preparing yourself for the divine appointments God provides in your home.

Next you meditate on the Word. You think about it, mull it over, ponder it... Don't just blow over difficult topics or hard to understand passages. Reading the Bible is not a race or an item on your daily check-off list. Slow down, drink in God's truth, and let it rest on your heart. It's one thing to know something, and another thing entirely to understand it well enough to explain it to a child. Take for instance, grace. Could you explain to a six-year old what the word means? Your child has no context for the term outside of church services and possibly your home. No one on the school playground or on the Disney Channel is talking about grace, but we sing "Amazing Grace" in services and read with joy from Ephesians 2:8 that we are, "...saved by grace through faith." Obviously it's a very important concept that your child needs to understand, but back to the question—do you understand grace enough to teach this beautiful gift of God to your kids? It takes thought and preparation to be ready to talk about concepts like this when the moment arises.[4]

Finally, you model the Word in your life. There's no better opportunity to stir up divine appointments than to act out what you believe in scripture. Little eyes are watching in the back seat when a rude driver cuts into your driving lane. Little minds are learning when you pray for the cashier at the grocery store who is obviously having a rough day. When you buy an extra hamburger in the drive-thru for a hungry man standing on the street, it is very likely to prompt a great discussion about how a Christ-follower should interact with the world in love and mercy. Every single day your children are forming their definition of "disciple of Christ" through your example. Scary thought, but absolutely true. That fact should drive us to our knees to plead for God's help every single day.

Each morning before school my family comes together by the front door to huddle up, pray, get encouragement for the day ahead, and devote ourselves to God. We call that time the "Before School Huddle", the "B.S.H.", or if we are being silly "The Burning Bsh." My youngest daughter just turned two, but

---

4   Don't panic if you can't answer this one. I'll actually address the concept of grace in chapter five and how to talk about it with your kids.

she absolutely loves to be a part of our huddle and join hands with the rest of the family. Of course she doesn't know how to pray, or even understand what is happening in that moment, but through modeling we are teaching her that daily she must rely on God's strength and devote herself to Godly choices. She doesn't get this today, and she won't get it tomorrow either. But one day she will... and it won't feel weird or strange when that time comes because it's been modeled for her a long, long time. Later when she hears my wife tell her how important it is to daily rely on God she'll think, "Yep. I know how to do that. My family has called out to God together in the morning for as long as I can remember."

As parents, we carry the heavy burden of modeling faith for the next generation. Our hits, and unfortunately our misses, are imprinting on our children what it means to be a disciple of Christ. Little eyes are watching and little ears are hearing more than we know. Are you living a life that gives you enough credibility to seize opportunities for spiritual development? Do your actions daily support the things you say you believe? You know this without me saying it... this stuff matters. If you want to have real, life-changing discussions with your child, then show them that Christ truly changed your life. Then you'll be ready to seize each divine appointment God orchestrates in your family.

CREATED OPPORTUNITIES

There are two people who are in charge of when spiritual growth happens in your child: The Holy Spirit and your child. That being said, there are things you can do in your home to raise the spiritual climate and foster faith talks. Before I introduce these strategies and techniques, I feel I must remind you again — accomplishing these things in your home is not the end... these are all means to an end. If you start doing all of these things at once, get overwhelmed, and then give up we are right back to where we started in chapter one. The goal of all these things is to allow you to speak life into your children and develop them spiritually on a consistent basis. The following suggestions merely serve that goal. Here are some things I've found that create opportunities for discipleship in my home:

SCRIPTURE MEMORY

I think my kids enjoy memorizing scripture more than anything else we do for spiritual formation. They enjoy the challenge of saying verses perfectly from memory without any mistakes and then testing mom and dad to see if we can do it too. As soon as we can all say a verse together, they are ready to start another one. I don't mind telling you... their young, fresh brains usually get it much faster than I do!

The key in my home is to keep it fun. One of our favorite scripture memory games is something we call the *One Word Circle.* One at a time each member of the family says one word of a verse until it's completed. If someone messes up, we just tell them what word he or she missed and start over. This is a great game before bed or even riding in the car. It gives you lots of repetition and you are working together as a team. I promise, by the end of the game everyone will know the verse you are working on perfectly.

Another way I help my kids learn scripture is by writing them on a marker board or a bathroom mirror with dry erase markers. Every day I erase a word or two and ask them to fill in the blanks from memory. I just keep erasing until the verse is gone from the board, but instead imprinted into their brains. You can use songs to help memorize verses, you can put motions to the words... There are a lot of different techniques out there, but the value of burying God's word in the heart of your child cannot be overstated. Check out his promise from Psalm 119:9-11

> *How can a young man keep his way pure? By keeping Your word. I have sought You with all my heart; don't let me wander from Your commands. I have treasured Your word in my heart so that I may not sin against You.*[5]

Don't we want our kids to treasure God's Word in their hearts? Of course we do! We can start them on that path now through scripture memory. And honestly... if our great goal is to make disciples through consistent faith talks at home (it is), this is about the easiest way I know to keep spiritual conversation going. You may be thinking, "Scripture memory is so old school..." Yep. I'm okay with that. We're not putting gold star stickers on Sunday School posters for every verse you learn anymore, but the practice is as relevant today as it was when you were a kid. It will still be relevant 1000 years from now if Jesus hasn't come back yet. In the future, families who are committed to exalting Christ in their floating houses will practice reciting Galatians 5:22 while the robot maid cleans the pizza printer and sets the wifi dinner plates back on their chargers. There is no power like speaking God's Word in your home, now and forever. Every second you spend on the scriptures is an opportunity for understanding and transformation in your children.

---

[5]   HCSB

HIGHLIGHTER TALKS

Confession: I love to highlight stuff. I feel like I'm retaining more when I swipe a color across some words that stand out to me when I read. Maybe I am... I don't know. I DO know that when I return to that material, it's much easier to find whatever it is I thought was important the first time around. I just look for the color.

I was thinking about this years ago when I gave my second son Abram a brand new Bible. Before giving it to him, I thought about my personal Bible and how much I loved it. When you are in the ministry you have a bunch of Bibles, but one in particular is MY Bible. It has gone to war with me through a myriad of spiritual battles. In one corner a scribbled date sits next to a verse I used to comfort coworkers the day the manager of the store I worked in died tragically in a car wreck. On another page an underlined verse reminds me of the time I decided to fight back with God's Word against the lust in my heart, even though I wasn't sure I could ever find victory. On another page I'd written three points to a sermon that I never wanted to forget. Over the course of many, many years I transformed my Bible into my own personal resource. I might not remember exactly the chapter and verse number of a certain text, but I could always find it. I could picture the words easily in my mind, where it was on the page, what color highlighter I used, etc., and flip to it fairly quickly.

I wanted that same familiarity for my son and his new Bible, so I came up with a small exercise we would do at night before bed called *Highlighter Talks*. First, I identified fifty verses I thought would be good for him to be able to find quickly. Then I broke up the verses into five categories and assigned each category a certain highlighter color:

- Yellow- God's Value for You
- Green- Living God's Way
- Orange- Talking with God
- Blue- The Bible's Importance
- Pink- Jesus' Work in Our Lives

Each night I challenged my son to look up one of the verses in his Bible, highlight it with the appropriate color, and then I asked the same question, "What does this verse mean to you?" Whatever he said was just fine with me. I wouldn't correct him, I would just let him think critically about the verse and form an explanation on his own. Then I would tell him what the verse means to me. We would then pray and say goodnight... that's it. We didn't need to read a fancy study or make anything out of uncooked macaroni. We just had short conversations about scripture before bed. It was an easy and quick way to end the night in the Word.

Well, I say we would have just a quick conversation, but that's not really true. We accomplished much more than that. First, my son transformed his new Bible into his own personal resource. He now could find scriptures in our predetermined subjects quickly and easily. Some nights, just for fun, I would send him on what I called, "Highlighter Hunts." He would flip through his Bible, find a scripture he'd already underlined, and we would talk about it all over again. Of course, it takes many years to really get a Bible worked in right, but my son was well on his way and learning how helpful it could be to mark it up, underline, and make notations.

We were also having spiritual conversations every single day. It was easy and consistent. My son got to listen to me think through and interact with scripture, and I got to hear him do the same. You just can't place a value on that. In this fun, low-pressure environment I fulfilled the command in Deuteronomy 6 to teach the Word of God to my children. The Kingdom of Heaven is found in small moments like this!

Check out the end of the book for my Highlighter Talk plan. I've listed all fifty verses from the five categories if you desire to use this strategy in your own home. Have fun!

OUTSIDE RESOURCES

If my phone goes missing and I hear giggling coming from the other room I can reasonably guess one of two things happened: either my children secretly snapped a picture of me picking my nose, or they've opened up *YouVersion Bible App for Kids* and are watching one of the excellently done interactive Bible stories. The app is just one of countless resources that can help keep faith front and center in your home. We live in a time of access. If someone wrote it, filmed it, or made it you can have it. Today. Usually in less than ten seconds. Most of this stuff isn't really worth our time (I'm looking at you cat videos), and some of it can be dangerous for a family trying to protect little eyes and ears, but if you are looking for something to help keep faith prominent in your home I promise you can find it.

Your church should be helping you with this. If not, talk with your minister or pastor about how important this is to you and ask what he or she would recommend. My church (The Church on Rush Creek in Arlington, Texas) gives families all sorts of resources to have spiritual conversations at home. We give them tools weekly to connect the lessons at church with discussion questions and fun activities, and we also give them material for special faith talks at strategic times (more on this in the next chapter). We deliver this content to families through books, handouts, links on an app, life group discussions, social media, etc. Here's my point... at The Church on Rush Creek if you desire to have a faith talk with your child we supply you with more than enough tools to make it happen. Most churches that serve families offer similar resources. Even if your church isn't actively equipping families, everything you need can be found fairly easy.[6] Now, it's up to you to go get them and start using them!

Seizing opportunities and creating opportunities are both ways to intentionally let faith flow down to your children. As God fills your heart with His truth, His love, His joy, and all other gifts only He can provide, your job as a parent is to let it overflow into your family. This doesn't happen by accident. You have to both look for opportunities and create moments to foster spiritual conversation in your home. But remember, checking off a list of completed activities is not your highest goal... the real objective is making disciples. Don't get derailed if you miss a day of Highlighter Talks or some devotional book you are using to stimulate spiritual growth... just get back on track and start again. You really can do this! You are exactly the right one to spiritually lead your family. God chose you and He can help you succeed. He can fill you with so much truth, love, and joy that it spills out of you all over your family each day.

He's really that good. Do you believe it?

---

6   Here are some of my favorite resources for families: books- What the Bible is All About: Bible Handbook for Kids, Jesus Wants All of Me, The Jesus Storybook Bible, The Hands On Bible online- YouVersion Bible App for Kids, Right Now Media

Chapter Wrap Up

- Every day we have opportunities to talk about faith in our home. We must intentionally look for these opportunities to let our faith flow down.

- According to the Shema, faith talks should happen constantly in the natural context of daily life.

- There are three types of faith talks we can use to lead our families in faith: seized opportunities, created opportunities, and special opportunities.

- God orchestrates divine appointments daily that we must seize in the moment to speak life into our children.

- Three disciplines help us get ready for teachable moments: reading the Word, meditating on the Word, and modeling the Word.

- Strategies like scripture memory, Highlighter Talks, and utilizing resources that stimulate faith conversations raise the spiritual climate of a home and create opportunities for spiritual teaching.

Talk About It

The following are questions to answer yourself or talk about in a group.

1. Why do you think seizing opportunities for faith talks in the normal routines of life is an effective strategy for spiritual leadership? Is it something that would work in your family life?

2. What steps are you taking (or plan to take) in order to ready yourself to seize every teachable moment to speak God's truth into your children?

3. What could cause you to miss teachable moments in your family life? How do you stay vigilant to intentionally watch for opportunities to seize the moment?

4. Did any of the ideas for creating spiritual conversation inspire you? Which of the suggestions, or other strategies you know of, will you attempt in your home?

5. What do you think are the benefits of reading and memorizing scripture with your family?

3

CELEBRATING MILESTONES

I cry during the Summer Olympics. There, I said it. Judge if you want.

It's just so incredibly moving to see elite athletes compete with all of their heart and soul, knowing that another shot won't come around for another four years. All their hours, days, months, even years of hard work come down to one moment (mere seconds in some events) of fierce, desperate competition against the entire world. My heart breaks with those who stumble. I shout and pump my fists with the victors. During a few weeks every fourth summer I get completely enthralled in sports I've never watch any other time, and I love every second of it.

Some of my favorite Olympic moments are the medal ceremonies. Watching gold medalists stand on the top podium with their awards glittering on proud chests while their trembling lips sing along to the national anthem and tears stream down flushed cheeks is beautiful to behold. Only the athletes know the price they paid to arrive at this moment, the work put in, the sacrifices made, the pleasures denied. But here, in the moment of victory, it's all worth it. You can see it in their bloodshot eyes. The joy in this ceremony comes gushing out in pure, overwhelming emotion that sweeps us all up in the celebration.

Recently in the news I've heard about athletes who were robbed of this ceremony. They competed with other Olympic athletes who cheated using performance-enhancing drugs. Those athletes got the gold medal podium moment, while Olympians who played by the rules watched from the side. Later, many of the athletes who used PEDs were caught and stripped of their medals, making way for the actual winners to receive their rightfully-earned awards. But the moment was over by then. For the rest of their lives the world will call these honest athletes Olympic medalists (and that's a big deal), but it's not quite the same getting a gold medal shipped to you in the mail, when the cheaters stood before adoring crowds and television cameras while people cheered and shouted their names. Tragically that moment was stolen from them.

> "Sometimes in order to teach big, important lessons it is necessary to create a special envoironment."

One speed walker from Australia decided he'd get his ceremony anyway. During the 2012 London Olympics, Jared Tallant crossed the finish line seconds after Russian athlete Sergey Kirdyapkin in the 50km walk. Later, Kirdyapkin was exposed as a cheater and his medal was stripped. It took four years, but finally in June of 2016 Tallant was awarded the gold medal for winning the event. In a video posted to Twitter, Tallant and his friends staged a ceremony of their own using a homemade wooden box to stand on, a medal brought forward on a bed pillow, and the Olympic Fanfare playing in the background. Later, Australia recognized Tallant's achievement with an actual ceremony in Melbourne. He might have been robbed of the moment during the 2012 Olympics, but he made sure he got a ceremony for his win.[7]

Ceremonies are important. They're meaningful times of celebration and reflection that mark special occasions. They can move us to appreciate reaching goals and motivate us to push for greater achievements. They are also unique chances to speak life and guidance into a child's life. In the hands of a spiritual leader, ceremonies can be powerful tools for developing a young life.

So far we've discussed seizing opportunities and creating opportunities for faith talks in the home. These two strategies are the most important and practical tools for parents to pass their faith down to their children. However, there is a third method for parents to instill faith in their children that is highly

---

7   John Salvado, "Jared Tallant Set to Receive Olympic Gold in Melbourne," espn. go.com.

effective— **special opportunities**. Special opportunities are unique and significant events on particular occasions for the purpose of instilling important life truths. Although special opportunities are much more formal than seized and created opportunities, and require much more planning and forethought, they can provide meaningful, life-changing lessons that stick long after the event is done. Because they're so effective, it's a smart idea to add special opportunities to our plan to let faith flow down to our children.

FAMILY CEREMONIES

Raising A Modern Day Night by Robert Lewis is an excellent book about the importance of fathers instilling manhood into their sons. One of the major themes in the book is the importance of ceremony in the home. As an example, he tells a story of a father who took his 16-year-old son John camping, but secretly planned a much more meaningful event. Lewis writes,

> *The Ford Explorer meandered slowly down the gravel road and halted on a wooden bridge near the Ouchita River near Friendship, Arkansas. On this cold November night, Bob Snider suddenly turned toward his 16-year-old son and asked, "John Snyder, do you want to become a man?"*

> *The question was certainly odd. John replied with a tentative "Uh-huh."*

> *Bob continued, "Well, then, I want you to get out and walk the rest of the way to the cabin."*

What a very confused John didn't know as he stepped out of the car was that his cousin was waiting to join him and share thoughts on overcoming fear while they walked. John's youth pastor joined them about a mile in and spoke to John about perseverance. Two other relatives came along next to hike with the men and talk about maturity and successful relationships. Finally, his grandfather met the group to tell John how important it is to learn to love. When the entire party made it to camp after walking over four miles, Bob began a highly symbolic ceremony that included personal stories about manhood from the respected men in John's life, a new Bible, and a steak dinner. This incredible ceremony took a great deal of planning and effort from Bob, but Lewis writes that it was well worth it.

> *The evening had a profound impact upon John. "that night, I got a big dose of what it means to be a man," he says. "I admire each of these men, and I want to be just like them. And every times I read my Bible, I*

remember the occasion."

Two years later, John Snider was one of two seniors at Pulaski Academy to win an award for "Excellence in Character." John has clearly taken to heart the lessons learned that evening and is actively seeking to follow the Lord Jesus Christ.[8]

Sometimes in order to teach big, important lessons it is necessary to create a **special environment** with the right people in the right place doing the right things. Bob changed the location, planned meaningful activities, and invited special people all for the purpose of teaching his son about manhood. Could he have used teachable moments to teach these lessons? Yes, and he probably did through consistent faith talks with his son. But by going to such lengths he communicated to John, "this is important. This is something you need to remember." And John took it all to heart. This is the power of ceremony.

But what if you don't have that kind of creativity to come up with big, life-changing ceremonies to impart truth into your child's life? Is there something out there to help you know what to do when to maximize your spiritual leadership? Actually, there is a brand new strategy for home leadership emerging all over the country that celebrates spiritual milestones children reach and turns them into concentrated life lessons. I didn't invent it, but I'm completely sold on its effectiveness. It's called *Faith Path*.

FAITH PATH
Several years ago a friend of mine recommended a book to me called *Shift* by Brian Haynes. God used the words on those pages to change the trajectory of my ministry calling. Let me explain.

At the time I was running pretty large church programs for children on Sunday mornings and Wednesday nights. Kids would come weekly for fun, fellowship, worship, Bible teaching, and small group discussion. Some good things happened... many children chose for themselves to follow Jesus and we celebrated those decisions with baptisms. Other kids found joy in serving and volunteered their time with local and global mission partners. New kids came weekly, families joined the church, we hosted big events, and everything worked like it was supposed to. There was one area where I was an utter fail-

---

8   Robert Lewis, Raising a Modern Day Knight (Carol Stream, Illinois: Tyndale House Publishers, 2007), 135-136.

ure, though—engaging parents in the spiritual life of their children. I tried a lot of strategies, but if anyone took part at all in these attempts, it was always the same parents who were already engaged in leading their homes and would come every time the church doors were open.[9] Most of my families merely dropped off their kids to the children's ministry and hoped our teaching stuck the rest of the week.

I needed something different— not another study or class or event that most of my parents would ignore—I needed a brand new idea. That's exactly what I found in the pages of Hayne's book. He didn't promote a new curriculum, class, or event for parents... all the things I tried and failed over the years. Instead, he proposed leading families to celebrate certain "spiritual milestones" every year or two, which would guide them to have the right conversations during appropriate seasons of life. He explained that I could take ceremonies my church already offered, like parent dedication services and children's baptism services, and link them into a spiritual pathway for families to walk together. Finally, this was something that made perfect sense to me. I didn't need to rely on an event or create yet another hour of weekly programming to help parents engage in spiritual leadership. I could equip parents right where they are to lead through special ceremonies. After reading *Shift*, I desperately desired to be a part of that strategy. Thankfully, after searching for a place where I could serve and help families celebrate milestones, I found the Church on Rush Creek in Arlington, Texas. The leaders in this great church share my passion for families and believe in the power of faith talks in the home.

This strategy is still emerging, but many are finding power in leading through milestones. It has several names around the country, but at Rush Creek we call it *Faith Path*. From birth to age 18 your family will celebrate thirteen milestones on the Faith Path that will accomplish three goals:

1. The Faith Path **identifies** the stage of development your child is entering and matches that with appropriate topics relevant to this season of life.
2. The Faith Path **celebrates** spiritual milestones in your child's life by recognizing big events and decisions that work toward shaping your child into a fully mature disciple of Christ.
3. The Faith Path **equips** parents to have specific talks relevant to the child's stage of development.

---

9   Praise the Lord for these families! I've done some lousy events during my time in ministry... I'm so thankful for church people who for some strange reason keep giving me chances.

Here's how it works— every year or so there is a specific subject to teach your child and milestone to celebrate based on his stage of development and spiritual readiness. On your child's birthday we invite you to engage in the correlating milestone by providing materials, videos, faith talk ideas, resources, church celebrations, and other helps to celebrate and lead through this important moment in your child's life. Let's take a look at the *Family Time Milestone* from the Faith Path as an example of what these particular special opportunities look like:

When your child turns four you are immediately invited to receive a big packet of materials that help you lead your family develop meaningful, consistent times together in spiritual conversation. Up until this age, faith talks suggested in the Faith Path have all been things to speak over your child (prayers, blessings, etc.), but because of growth and maturation he has now graduated to participate and interact with your spiritual leadership. This is a big change that is worth celebrating! The materials include a booklet that stresses the importance of being intentional with your kids, some fun ideas on how to turn ordinary life events like movie nights and rides in the car into teachable moments, a commitment to sign that expresses your intention to be consistent in leading your family, and recommended resources for further exploration. You also get a card with a link to a video on the importance of family time in the home, stickers to place on a calendar every time you schedule a family time, and a plan for a creative faith talk in your home. The plan is called "Just Like Air" and it uses the air in a balloon to teach kids that God is always there, even when we can't see Him. Fun, cool, easy… just the way I like it! Everything you need to develop and practice a consistent and effective family time can be found inside this milestone packet.

This Family Time Milestone is attached to a church celebration that we invite families to periodically. During the event we play games together, watch short movies, pretend to ride in cars, and do all sorts of other fun things; while at the same time modeling how to turn all those moments into family faith talks.

Not every milestone includes church celebrations, but several do. Parent Dedication is a milestone on the Faith Path; so is our children's baptism service. When our seniors reach high school graduation, we call it Launch and recognize this significant milestone in front of the entire church. In all our Faith Path milestones we want to celebrate with families, equip them for that season in their child's spiritual development, and then provide special opportunities for meaningful growth. Here's a rundown of each milestone along the path all the

way through high school graduation:
- Parent Dedication (recommended focus: birth to 2)
- Blessing (Recommended focus: age 3+)
- Family Time (Recommended focus: age 4+)
- Prepare to Lead Your Child to Christ (age will vary)
- Prayer (Recommended focus: age 6+)
- Bible (Recommended focus: age 7+)
- Worship (Recommended focus: age 8+)
- Giving & Serving (Recommended focus: age 9+)
- Preparing for Adolescence (Recommended focus: age 11+)
- Purity (Recommended focus: age 13+)
- Rite of Passage (Recommended focus: age 16+)
- Launch (Recommended focus: age 18+)[10]

If your church doesn't have something similar to the Faith Path, don't sweat it. Haynes, the family pastor who invented the strategy and helped me understand a new way of reaching families, has written a book for parents to accomplish these things without the aid of a church. You can find his book, *The Legacy Path*, on Amazon or wherever you buy books. Remember, this strategy is not a church program or a weekly service. It simply helps you know what your child needs now, gives you some ideas to meet those needs through special opportunities, and shows you where you are going next in your child's spiritual development. You can do this on your own!

Special opportunities are incredibly effective tools for speaking life in to your children. Ceremonies and unique events help create meaningful environments for lessons that stick. Although most of our spiritual leadership investment involves teachable moments and daily conversations, special opportunities can help us turn spiritual milestones into celebration and motivation for continued growth.

---

10   The curriculum for the Faith Path was produced and distributed by Homepointe Inc. To find out more visit their website at drivefaithhome.com.

Chapter Wrap Up

- While seizing opportunities and creating faith talks are the main tools for letting faith flow down, special opportunities of celebration and teaching are also very effective to stimulate spiritual conversations.

- Ceremonies are formal events that recognize achievements and deliver important lessons to children. Families can use ceremonies at home to mark occasions and motivate growth.

- Creating special environments help children understand the importance of the message you want to convey.

- It's important to celebrate spiritual milestones children reach, while at the same time preparing them to reach the next one.

Talk About It

The following are questions to answer yourself or talk about in a group.

1. What are some of the most special ceremonies you've taken part in? What made them special?

2. What spiritual milestones are worth celebrating in your child's life?

3. Did your parents or guardians use ceremony as a spiritual leadership tool when you were growing up If so, how? If not, do you think it would have been meaningful for you?

4. Put yourself in John's place (the teenager from the camping story). How do you think that event shaped him as a man later in life?

5. Out of the three strategies for letting faith flow down (seized opportunities, created opportunities, and special opportunities), which is the most natural for you to use in your home? Which do you think is most effective? Which, if any, do you need to adopt?

PART TWO

FAITH
FOR
CHILDREN

4

YOUR CHILD IS NOT YOU

I'm going to open this chapter with a statement so provocative, so radical that it just may change the way you interact with children forever.

Your child is not you.

Okay, so maybe not *that* radical, but I'm convinced many people who should know better somehow forget this obvious fact. It comes out in the things parents say to me sometimes:

"I'm not sure my daughter can really understand the Bible. When I was a kid I was confused about…"

"I don't understand why my kids aren't as heartbroken as I am over our recent loss. They haven't even cried about…"

"My son is asking really deep questions about what it means to be a Christian, but I know he's not ready to choose for himself to follow Jesus. I didn't make that decision myself until I was…"

Without thinking about it, parents fall into this trap. We project our own history, feelings, and experiences onto our children, forgetting they are writing their own unique story with God who is intimate and personal with every single one of His children. Just because you were mistakenly baptized at a young age before you truly understood what it meant to follow Jesus, doesn't mean that your child can't be serious about his or her decision. Just because your child displays emotion differently than you doesn't make his or her feelings any less legitimate. You are absolutely called to lead your child in every way, but don't be scared or intimidated if their path is somehow divergent from yours. That's actually a good sign. It means your child is not simply parroting your life, but rather allowing God to mold her into His unique and special masterpiece. If you are committed to leading your child spiritually, this is an incredibly important truth to understand.

I knew very early that my oldest son Roe is very different than me, but that didn't make it any easier to accept. I loved sports as a kid. I played football and baseball for my school teams and watched SEC football religiously every Saturday in the fall. Honestly, my identity was a little too wrapped up in being an athlete. My friend groups revolved around sports, my schedule was controlled by sports, and all my dreams for the future featured sports. I can admit it now… athletics were an idol in my life.

On the day I discovered my first child was going to be a son, I immediately began dreaming new dreams. I imagined myself in a coach's shirt, blowing a whistle, and leading my son and his team through drills. I daydreamed about long hours of catch in the front yard. If you asked me, I knew enough to say the right things like, "I'll be a fan of whatever my son is into," or, "my son can be whatever he wants to be," but deep down I really never imagined a world where my child didn't love sports. It was who I was, so it would most certainly be who he would become.

I started Roe on baseball early. We would go out in the front yard with a soft bat and ball and I would pitch to him. He caught on quickly and before long he could hit the ball fairly well. We would have fun and laugh and just enjoy being out together. Roe liked playing around and acting silly far more than the actual sport of baseball, but I figured most kids were like that at his age and at some point competitiveness would kick in and focus him on the game. As soon as he was old enough I signed him up for little league. I didn't know it, but this was the beginning of the end of his baseball career. I quickly discovered Roe really didn't care about the game. He liked playing with me in the front yard, but the sport itself didn't really rock his boat. To his credit, he gave baseball a shot for a couple of years. Right before the last game of his final year, my wife Noël asked him, "Roe, are you ready for your last game of the season?" He replied, "It's the last game of my life!" We got the picture.

Now I know the lesson here is obvious: Let the kid be who he wants to be. Support him no matter what he's into. Yeah, yeah, yeah... I know. But this was really my first crisis as a parent. Remember, I learned to navigate the world through sports. Sports helped me make friends. Sports (wrongly) defined my identity. Almost every day I went to a practice or game of some sort. It was a huge part of my childhood and now my son was choosing an alternate path. In some ways I had no idea how to help him walk this different road.

Today Roe is a teenager and I marvel at his gifts. He is a cartoonist and his cartoons absolutely crack me up. He creates videos and other projects just for fun, serves in the nursery of our church, plays trombone in his school band, acts in plays, and stays at the top of his class in every school subject. He's even giving sports a try again by joining the school wrestling team. He still won't watch football with me on Saturdays (I'm holding out hope for that), but he has turned into an outstanding young man. Most importantly he loves Jesus and boldly makes choices to honor Him daily. In another departure, he chose to follow Jesus at a much younger age than I did. He is serious about the Lord and committed to his faith.

Roe is not me. His story is unfolding much differently than mine, and I am so thankful for that. When I died to my preconceived notions of who my first son would become, he was free to be exactly who God made him to be. He's not perfect, and we still have a lot of shaping and molding to do before he leaves my house, but Roe has taught me so much about living as an individual and being comfortable in my own skin. The path he walks makes me a better person.

So how do we keep from projecting our feelings, history, and expectations on our children? As we let our faith flow down through seized opportunities for faith talks daily, created opportunities for spiritual instruction, and special times of memorable lessons we must always consider the child's individuality. As a parent you have to value your kids' interests, culture, and development. That's why you're the best spiritual leader for your family... no one can know your child as well as you!

INTERESTS

Do you know what your child is into? Have you ever played her video games or listened to her music? Do you know her favorite characters in movies or books? When you share in the interests of your child you silently communicate, "I care about what you care about. I'm into you." You are also collecting points of connection you can use to communicate with your child. My kids love it when I sit on the floor and play video games with them or go outside with them to enjoy the backyard. During our play their thoughts and feelings spill out of their mouths almost without them realizing it. They tell me about the highs and lows of their day, struggles they are having with classmates, questions on their heart, and whatever else flashes through their brains. Sure, I could come home from work and zone out. Honestly sometimes I want to. But when I connect with my children through the things they love I get a glimpse into their passions and gain credibility as their leader. There's an old saying, "Quality time is better than quantity time." Guess what… that saying is ridiculous and stupid. In the case of your children, quantity time IS quality time and visa versa. There is no quick fix to replace spending time with your kids, enjoying the things they love.

This probably means you will have to expand your interests. A couple of my children went through a claymation phase. Can you imagine how tedious it is to take a clay sculpture your kids made, place it in a background, take a picture, move it a fraction of an inch, take another picture, repeat this action a hundred times, and then edit the whole thing for roughly 15 seconds of video? Honestly, they enjoyed it so much that I ended up enjoying it too. I thought long and hard about how to make our movies better, how to pull off certain shots in their story, make the transitions cleaner… When the phase ended I was a little sad. Every now and then I ask, "Don't you guys want to make claymation videos anymore?" but they've moved onto other interests. I didn't start out loving making these videos, but I loved my kids, so it really wasn't that hard to learn to enjoy what they enjoy.

CULTURE

Here's another question: Do you truly understand the cultural differences between you and your children? Modern children are living in different realities than we grew up with. Some of these realities are positive… consider this: Kids today have unprecedented access to more information and entertainment than at any point in history. For example, according to a 2014 study this is what happens every **minute**:

- Facebook users share almost 2.5 million pieces of content
- 300,000 Tweet are posted on Twitter
- 220,000 new photos are loaded into Instagram
- YouTube users upload 72 hours of video
- Almost 50,000 apps are downloaded from Apple

- Over 200 million messages are sent by email[11]

That's a mind-blowing amount of content! In fact, estimates suggest that 2.5 quintillion bytes of data are produced every single day.[12] Do you know how much information that is? Me either... but I'm guessing a lot. And all of it is a click away for our kids. These children are digital natives who can receive and process data at lightning fast speeds. Science is even beginning to discover that the new generation's brains work differently from those of us born earlier to accommodate the onslaught of information.[13]

Access doesn't stop with the internet. Modern kids have unbelievable opportunities at their fingertips. If they want to play a sport—any sport— there's an organized league available to them. If they want to watch a movie they can stream it instantly. If they want to communicate with their friends, they can do that too; right this second. There are very few opportunities children have to wait for anymore.

And of course we have to talk about the harmful things accessible to our children. I've had more than one friend tell me, "If iPhones were around when I was a kid, I would have gotten myself into a lot of trouble!" The web is everywhere... on phones, on game consoles, smart TVs, tablets, etc. and it's dangerous for little eyes and ears. A 2016 article in Time Magazine by Belinda Luscombe reports that last year people watched a combined 4,392,486,580 hours of porn on just one specific website.[14] I'll do the math for you... that equals over 180 million days of online consumption, the equivalent to over 501,000 years of watching harmful videos. Peggy Orenstein, in that same magazine issue, brings the statistics a little closer to home by revealing that 40% of children between the ages of 10 and 17 have seen explicit material online, and by the time kids reach college those averages have increased significantly. According to a study of 800 college students, 90% of guys and 33% of girls had viewed pornography within the previous year.[15] Companies are making apps specifically to help kids hide their viewing history from their parents. Other apps make it easy for kids to bully other kids anonymously, coax young boys and girls to post inappropriate pictures of themselves, or

11   Susan Gunelius, "The Data Explosion in 2014 Minute by Minute- Infograph," aci.info.
12   Daniel Price, "Surprising Facts and Stats about the Big Data Industry," cloudtweaks. com.
13   Jim Taylor Ph.D., "How Technology is Changing the Way Children Think and Focus," Psychologytoday.com.
14   Belinda Luscombe, "Porn and the Threat to Virility," Time Magazine (April 11, 2016): 43.
15   Peggy Orenstein , "How Porn is Changing a Generation of Girls," Time Magazine (April 11, 2016): 47.

do other destructive things online. And the internet isn't the only problem, either. Kids are exposed to graphic violence, profanity, sexual content, and crudeness in their video games, music, and movies. All of this filth is not just benign... What I mean is, the bad stuff isn't just sitting in the dark corner of the internet for those who go searching for it. The filth is coming after our children aggressively. Many kids who see pornography online, see it for the first time by accident.

So how do you parent a kid growing up in this time of access and exposure? One thing we must strongly consider is how to protect our families from the pervasive culture. The absolute worst thing you can do is sit back and remain ignorant. If you believe your child's experience growing up is just like yours and that you can raise them just like your father or mother raised you, you're not paying attention. Our kids live in a complicated world and they need parents who are willing to fight for them.

About 2500 years ago there was a Jewish man named Nehemiah living in exile in Persia. News reached him that his hometown's wall had crumbled and that his people, God's people, were in danger from the surrounding countries. This information broke his heart and placed a calling on his life to do something about it, so he traveled home to Jerusalem to fix the wall, organize the people, and restore the city. The work started well, certain families took ownership of portions of the wall, and they all worked hard. The Ammonites, Ashdodites, and the Arabs living around Jerusalem however didn't like this restoration project one bit. These people from neighboring countries loved having easy access and free reign over the city, so they taunted, jeered, and attacked the Israelites working on the wall. Nehemiah stationed guards to cover the workers night and day, but the attacks were relentless. When the Israelites were at their lowest point, Nehemiah stood up and gave an inspiring challenge recorded in Nehemiah 4:14. His words then are completely relevant to us today:

> "Our kids live in a complicated world and they need parents who are willing to fight for them."

> Don't be afraid of them. Remember the great and awe-inspiring Lord, and fight for your countrymen, your sons and daughters, your wives and homes.[16]

16   HCSB

We can't ever forget that our sons and daughters are under attack right now. The culture is invading our homes and it's driven by a world that actively works to undermine the Christian values, morals, and ideals we believe in. A parent who fights for the hearts of children doesn't necessarily shut out the culture—it is a great thing for kids to learn how to love, understand, and interact with all kinds of different people—rather, he or she finds the bravery to have tough and honest conversations, sets boundaries to protect the family from harmful things with tools like internet filters and age restrictors, and coaches children how to make wise choices to honor God above all else.

We must also consider less obvious ramifications of today's culture. Think about this—children today have no idea how to be bored. They are entertained every moment of every day and this condition flies in the face of important spiritual disciplines like prayer and meditation. You can quote Lamentations 3:26 to today's young people, "It is good to wait quietly for deliverance from the Lord," but they have no ability or practice at being patient and still. They need adults to model and coach them on this in a way children from previous generations who spent hours and hours daydreaming and playing make-believe never did.

Mom and dad, if your head is buried in the sand, it's time to lift it up. We must know and engage the culture so we can help our children navigate it. Are these scary times we are living in? Maybe… it depends on your perspective. Either way, these are the times God planned before the creation of the world for us to parent these children. Modern culture needs an invasion of new disciples for Christ rising from our homes and impacting this different, changing world for the Kingdom of God.

GROWTH

Probably the easiest way to forget the difference in children and adults lies in the area of development. Simply put, kids do not learn like adults learn. I've talked to many well-meaning parents, teachers, and small group leaders who believed their objective during a lesson is to get kids to sit quietly, listen to a Bible lesson, and participate in class discussion. That method may work for adults (debatable), but it doesn't work at all for kids. These leaders have subconsciously tried to turn kids into little adults and teach them the way they themselves like to learn, but developmentally they are miles apart.

To understand the developmental needs of children, let's start with movement and noise. Generally, adults enjoy quiet, peaceful places to think and process information. Kids... not so much. Play is the tool of greatest learning in most childhood stages. Children need to stand, move, experience, and do. This is how they explore the world around them. Maybe you think best in a quiet room, free of distractions. Your child interacts with the world by creating the distractions. Noise and activity are not always signs that your child isn't engaged mentally with what is going on in the room, even if it feels that way to you.

My wife and I value taking our children to corporate worship with us every week. They go to their own small groups that are age appropriate first, and then they come with us into the service. I'm under no delusion that my elementary age children can fully understand and engage with everything happening around them. They wiggle. They draw pictures. When they were younger they crawled under chairs and talked too loud and fell asleep. Why do we value this commotion? Because when they see their mom and me worship with hands raised they learn how to celebrate God with song. When they see us take notes and follow along with the sermon in our Bibles they learn to value the spoken Word of God. I love catching my children drawing on their worship folder something the pastor just talked about or whispering a question to mom about something we just read in scripture. Learning is happening, even if it's not my kind of learning.

Another aspect to consider is the development of a child's brain. Every functioning brain has a part in the front called the "frontal lobe." This part of the brain is responsible for controlling emotions, impulses, cause and effect relationships, thinking abstractly, and other similar processes. The problem is that the frontal lobe doesn't work all that well in children. In fact, the frontal lobe really doesn't function much until adolescence, and isn't fully formed until around age 25.[17] Have you ever wondered why teenagers make such terrible choices? One reason is because they are most likely using another part of their brain to make decisions- the amygdala. This part makes instinctive, emotional decisions almost impossible to ignore without the help of the frontal lobe. So there you go... there are real, scientific reasons your teenager may be impulsive and irrational, but it doesn't make that skull tattoo any easier to look at I'm afraid.

---

17   Sara B. Johnson Ph.D, M.P.H, Robert W. Blum. M.D., Ph.D., and Jay N. Giedd, M.D., "Adolescent Maturity and the Brain: The Promise and Pitfalls of Neuroscience Research in Adolescent Helath Policy," J Adolesc Health. (Sept. 2009): 45(3): 216-221.

Without the help of the frontal lobe, young children are left seeing the world in concrete, black and white terms. This has huge implications on matters of faith and how children understand things as opposed to adults. Take justification for instance. We learn in the book of Romans that all have sinned (3:23), the punishment for sin is death (6:23), but Jesus will save every person who will, "confess with our mouth, 'Jesus is Lord,' and believe in your heart that God raised Him from the dead (10:9)." Look at all the abstract concepts in this extremely important, foundational teaching:

- The punishment for sin is death- What do you think this means to a child who thinks only in concrete terms? Children are likely to believe they will physically die because they pushed their brother off the swing on the playground. Or they may say to themselves, "I lied to my parents last week and my heart is still beating... this stuff must not be true."

- Jesus will save me- From what? How do kids understand their soul is in eternal danger when they feel fine here on earth?

- To be saved you must confess, "Jesus is Lord."- "Oh... so all I have to do is say some magic words? I can do that!"

- Believe in my heart- Believing really isn't a problem for kids. They believe all sorts of things, especially when adults they trust tell them it's true. Is that what this verse means? Kids believe in Jesus and Santa and that when they pull the covers up tightly over their head at night it keeps bad men from attacking with chainsaws.

Now don't worry, I'm going to circle back in chapter five and talk specifically about how to talk to your kids about salvation, but this issue opens up a can of worms doesn't it? The concepts above are just a small sampling of the abstract concepts central to our faith, yet very difficult for a child to understand. That doesn't mean children can't grasp the understanding necessary for salvation and discipleship... they absolutely can. What it means is that we can't assume kids are making certain connections mentally that may be easy for us old fogies. We have to help them reach the right conclusions. Let me give you an example of what I mean:

When I share the gospel with a group of children I always start with God's great love for them. I'll say something like this, "God loves you so much. He knew your name before you were born. He knows the color of your eyes, how many hairs you have on your head, and He wants to be so close to you. He wants to share His love with you forever, stay so close to you, and for nothing to ever come between you. Being close to God means life. When you are right by His side He fills you with life and light. Being away from God means spiritual death and darkness."

Now why would I bring up death and darkness at this point? Because kids can't understand why they need Jesus unless they understand their deep, unseen need for restoration with God. When I explain next that sin drives a wedge between us and God using Romans 6:23- *"For the wages of sin is death, but the gift of God is eternal life in Christ Jesus our Lord,"*[18] I need kids to understand exactly what this "spiritual death" means. So I give them a concrete association in order to understand an abstract concept: close with God means life, distance from God means death.

Kids brains are amazing. They can soak up new information quickly, like a sponge soaks up water. They really can get big concepts, but as a parent we must make the connections for them. We have to help them understand that loving your neighbor means serving homeless men and women downtown, not just hope they figure it out themselves. We have to explain to them that when Jesus says in Luke that the shepherd will leave 99 sheep behind to find one, he really means that He came to bring people in darkness through sin back into the presence of God. They can get this, but we must connect the dots.

Here's a quick reference guide to know what your child needs from birth through teen years for faith development. These aren't hard and fast rules since every child progresses at a different pace. Still, this will give you a good idea about what to concentrate on through every stage.

BABIES- FEEL THE FAITH

Babies need to feel loved and safe at home and at church. They need to know you will provide for their every need, be a source of hugs and encouragement, and keep them from harm. They are forming their first impressions of the world and will begin to understand love and trust from their relationship with you. One day, when they learn that we are "children of God" who is our Holy Father, they will most likely attribute His characteristics to how they feel about you.

---

18   HCSB

PRESCHOOL- BUILD THE FAITH

Once children develop communication skills, you can begin to introduce simple words of faith and spiritual concepts. In this stage you are constructing a foundation of understanding that will be built upon from here on out. Good things to do include singing simple songs, introducing major Bible characters and stories, and making associations. Say things like, "point to your nose. God made your nose," or, "The Bible is God's book. It is very important." These simple truths introduce God's presence in every aspect of life and start early to build the beginnings of a faith foundation.

YOUNGER ELEMENTARY- DEFINE THE FAITH

In this stage children need to begin moving toward better understanding of concepts central to salvation, morality, and God's interaction with His people. Most first graders can understand terms like sin, grace, forgiveness, and discipleship if led well by a caring, conscientious adult. Young children can also learn the importance of making wise choices and loving their neighbor. Disciplines like prayer and Bible reading can also be introduced as a personal responsibility.

OLDER ELEMENTARY- EXPLORE THE FAITH

It is very good for children to begin practicing their faith as early as possible, but it becomes vital in the preteen years. Children who get "hands on" with community mission projects, evangelistic conversations, journaling, or praying with friends are much more likely to adopt these practices as a way of life. Talking about living out faith with kids is a great thing to do, but actually doing some of these things will accelerate spiritual growth like nothing else.

YOUNGER TEEN- LIVE THE FAITH

There is a major shift that comes with breaking through adolescence. Because these kids have developed new capacities, expectations should rise and motivations should become more personalized. As an example, we tell younger children to love others because God commands it. Teenagers however can understand that love is not something we do, but something we are because God is love and His Spirit lives within us. Young teens should also begin to truly understand what having a relationship with Christ truly means on an intimate level and begin fostering it daily through real connection.

OLDER TEEN- OWN THE FAITH

This is the great hope... that by the time teens begin thinking about the future and independence, following Christ is not something you need to encourage anymore. Rather, it's a part of their personal character. To get to this goal, young people need to ask tough questions, make hard choices, and have experiences that lead them to own their faith journey. Kids don't reach owner-ship by sitting in a classroom; they find it in crisis. They find it on the mission field or in the pages of their worn out Bibles. Students in this stage should sit awhile with big, giant questions and parents should resist cliché, flippant answers. Older teens should take risks following Christ that make mom and dad uncomfortable. This is the path to ownership.

Your child is not you. Don't let this fact scare you… embrace it! Celebrate that your child has different interests, lives in a different culture, and is develop-mentally different from you. Be a student of their individuality and allow God to write their story instead of forcing your expectations down their throat. Your role as a parent is not to reproduce yourself. Your role is to lead your child to glorify God. That only happens when your child becomes exactly who God designed him to be.

Chapter Wrap Up

- To keep from projecting our own feelings, history, and expectations on our children we must consider their interests, culture, and level of maturity.

- Learning to love what our kids love shows them we care about them and value spending time with them.

- Kids are growing up in difficult times. Their access and exposure means we must do everything possible to protect and help them navigate the changing world we live in.

- Children learn and think differently than adults. This fact has direct ramifications on their understanding of biblical truth.

Talk About It

The following are questions to answer yourself or talk about in a group.

1. What limiting beliefs from your spiritual history are you tempted to project onto your children? How do you guard against giving into this temptation?

2. How are your children different than you? Is it easy or hard for you to celebrate these differences?

3. What are your kids into? What do you enjoy doing together?

4. What do you need to do in your home to protect your children from the pervasive culture?

5. After identifying your child's stage on the above faith development guide, what do you need to concentrate on to help your child grow spiritually in this season of life?

NAKED BEFORE GOD

There's one question parents ask me more than any other. I actually really like this question. When I hear it I know these moms and dads care at least a little bit about spiritually leading their children and have a sense of their responsibility. The question can take different forms, but in essence it's always the same:

"Is it normal for my kid to enjoy being naked so much?"

Just kidding, that's not the question (Had you worried with my chapter title, didn't I?). I am going to talk a lot about nudity later in this chapter, but in a slightly different context.[19] No, here's the real question:

"How do I know when my child is ready to become a follower of Jesus?"

As you love God and His commands, faith should flow out of you in the form of seized opportunities, created opportunities, and special opportunities onto your children. Still, that doesn't mean that your efforts automatically turn your children into Christ-followers. There must be an entry point into the life of faith... a moment when your child decides for himself that he wants to choose Jesus as the King of his life over everything else. This is a huge, life-changing decision that can be somewhat intimidating for parents. They worry about

---

19   If you were wondering... yep. Totally normal.

age, understanding, maturity, and a whole host of other factors.

When parents ask me, "How do I know when my child is ready?" I give them two

answers. One is the most accurate and the other is the most practical. Let's start with the truest answer and then work back from there:

ANSWER #1

You can't.

Maybe I should expound on that answer...

You can't know the heart of your child, but the Holy Spirit can. You can see outward signs and observe outward expressions, but you can't be 100% sure you know what is going on in the places you can't see. That means it's incredibly important to draw close to the God who sees our hearts and depend on Him to guide you.

Children want to "say the prayer" or "ask Jesus into their hearts" for lots of different reasons.[20] Some kids have seen their friends get celebrated for making a decision to follow Christ. Others are dying to know what communion tastes like. Still others have been convinced by their grandmothers that they should be able to give their lives to Jesus because, "everyone else in the family did around your age." Really there is only one reason for anyone to become a follower of Christ. Jesus said it Himself in John 6:44:

> No one can come to Me unless the Father who sent Me draws him, and I will raise him up on the last day.[21]

Salvation starts with God. It is never our idea. God calls people to Himself whenever He chooses in any way He sees fit. His call on a young heart can look very emotional, very thoughtful, or somewhere in between. Some children who are not ready to make a serious commitment to Christ can wax eloquent all day about their need for God... especially those well-educated with a background in Christian instruction. Others have no idea how to communicate the call on their hearts, even though that call is real and legitimate.

---

20   I know this terminology just set off alarm bells in some of your heads. Chapter 5 is all about leading your child to salvation. I promise I'll do my best to clear up some misleading things we tell children about following Christ... Hang with me.
21   HCSB

For these reasons we can't simply rely on the responses we see with our eyes and hear with our ears to gauge the readiness of children for the gospel. Reactions are helpful clues, but they can also mislead. For this reason parents **must** rely on the Holy Spirit's leadership for this momentous first decision.

Again we go back to the teaching of the Shema—love God first, and then lead your family. It sounds so simple, but it's easy to get the order mixed up. Many parents are so scared to lead children through this decision incorrectly... I get it. This is serious business. The on ramp into a life of faith is important to get right the first time around. But here is something I believe passionately: You are the God-ordained spiritual leader of your child, and He equips His followers to fulfill the tasks He puts before them. That means we can trust God will help us know the right pace to adopt for leading our children into salvation. Our job is to pray, seek, listen, and obey.

> *He who calls you is faithful, who also will do it.* —1 Thessalonians 5:24 HCSB

> *"You will seek Me and find Me when you search for Me with all your heart.* — Jeremiah 29:13 HCSB

And so we pray and seek the Lord and ultimately trust His timing and His plans for our children to find the narrow road. For some the wait is excruciating. Some parents want so badly for their kids to be a part of the Kingdom of God they try to force them into making a commitment before they are ready to take ownership of the decision. Kids who love to please their parents are especially susceptible to going through the motions of salvation because they believe it will make their parents happy, rather than because God is calling them to Himself.

Other parents feel like their children are racing toward Jesus without considering enough the ramifications of these decisions on the rest of their lives. These parents want their kids to slow down and ask more questions about things they are already very sure about. Maybe these children are completely comfortable with the pace of their maturation, but it's way too fast for mom and dad.

There are dangers to both approaches. Parents who want to slow down their children risk frustrating their kids and keeping them from answering the call of God on their heart. Parents who want to speed up their children risk confusion and manipulation that must be undone when the call of God truly comes. The answer to both issues is to let the Holy Spirit set the pace. He alone knows what is best for your child. Your best hope is to seek His activity in your family and join Him in the work.

ANSWER #2

So, I told you there were two answers I give parents who want to know when their kids are ready to follow Jesus… trusting the Holy Spirit is the best possible action you can take to ensure spiritual readiness. However, there is an answer that is a little more practical. It's not foolproof, but it can be a guide for you along the way while you are seeking God for your child's salvation. Here it is—**Your child must understand that he or she has a deep need.**

There's a lot of terminology that people use for this awareness of need. Some might say a child is "under conviction." Others might say that, "Jesus is knocking on the door of her heart." Theology textbooks would say the child is beginning to realize her "total depravity." Whatever the words used for when the calling comes, kids should understand there is a void that must be filled by something outside of themselves. This understanding is urgent and personal and important to a child when it truly emerges.

Now, notice that I didn't say your child must understand he or she has a deep need **for Jesus.** Ultimately that is the need that must be met, but children may not connect their need with Jesus' salvation on their own. They make think they need to get baptized, start acting right, or get away from bad influences. All those things may be symptoms of the craving in their hearts, but it's our job as parents to connect their perceived need with the real solution- the free gift of salvation in Christ.

Sometimes parents will hesitate to talk about sin with their kids. They don't want them to feel bad or ever think they are "sinners." A concept like that just doesn't vibe with the modern, "everybody is great, so be proud of who you are," mindset. This view that seems so compassionate and kind actually stands in stark contrast to the teachings of the Bible. I tell my kids they need Jesus as soon as they can understand words. I never want my children to believe that salvation in Christ is a birthright or an inheritance. It's not. Until kids know they are personally responsible for the sin that separates them from God, salvation cannot begin in young hearts.

Again, outward expression of conviction isn't a foolproof sign that God is calling a child. Churched kids in particular get pretty adept at admitting their sins... our ministers and children's leaders train them pretty well on this theological understanding. But some acknowledgment of personal need must occur before salvation can take place. This can serve as an affirmation of where the Holy Spirit is leading you as a parent. Art Murphy, one of my favorite experts on this subject, helps us know what to look for in his book *The Faith of a Child:*[22]

> "Listen to how he talks about becoming a Christian. Is there an urgency on his part? Does he have a personal desire to talk about salvation? Sometimes children who are familiar with the Christian language or have been raised in a Christian environment have an attitude of "Sure, why not," "I guess so," or "It sounds like a good idea to me." This may be a sign that the child has not reached a time of conviction. When a child is serious about his commitment to Christ, he should have an attitude of "I need to do this. I must ask Christ to come into my life."[23]

Our great need for Jesus stems from the wreckage of sin in our lives. The trouble started in the Garden of Eden long, long ago. Over time, cultures changed, generations came and went, empires rose and fell; but no matter where or when sin has been present to drive a wedge between people and God. It will be this way until Jesus comes back, and this is the singular source of our need.

KNOWING WE ARE NAKED

A few years ago I was talking about all this stuff with my pastor friend, Darren Miley. He told me he once read that the "age of accountability" (the moment children are responsible for their sins) occurred when a child recognizes his or her own nakedness. The thought here is children tend to run around the house (or the yard, or the park, or wherever they can get away from their parent's watchful eye) in their birthday suits without any hint of shame or embarrassment.[24] At some point in their maturation something clicks in their brains and they have a strong desire to hide themselves. At first I laughed off this answer... and please be assured I still don't believe in an age of ac-

---

22   Art Murphy, The Faith of a Child (Chicago, Illinois: Moody, 2000), 77.
23   Art Murphy's chapter on the readiness of a child for salvation is packed full of awesome information. In fact, he gives 5 questions to ask during this time that are just too good not to include in this book. See Art Murphy's Five Questions in Appendix 2 for more on this.
24   I reeeeeeeeally want to tell some stories here, but I'm pretty sure my children would kill me. If you have children I bet you have stories too. I guess we'll just have to save the embarrassing stuff for our wedding toasts.

countability, nor do I believe the physical desire to cover up your body is any indication of spiritual readiness, but actually there is a parallel between a child's need for Jesus and the awareness of nakedness. To find it, let's go back to the Garden of Eden where the problem of sin began.

In Genesis 2 we learn what early life was like for Adam and Eve, the first people ever created by God. Adam had the job of caring for the garden and naming all the animals. He and Eve had one rule to follow: don't eat the fruit from the tree in the middle of the garden. They could have *ANYTHING ELSE THEY DESIRED...* just not that one thing. Adam and Eve enjoyed closeness with God and each other during this time that was pure and holy and completely unhindered by anything that could disrupt their fellowship. How did the writer of Genesis describe this unadulterated relationship?

> *Both the man and his wife were naked, yet felt no shame.*
> – Genesis 2:25 HCSB

Adam and Eve had no sense that they had to hold anything back from God or each other. No self-esteem issues kept them from putting their true selves out front and center. The love between them was perfect, free from disparaging attitudes, and unrestricted in giving and receiving. The lushness and extravagance of the garden is not why Eden was paradise, it was this complete and unabashed intimacy the new humans shared with God.

And then the serpent came and messed everything up. Well, not so much him, but Adam and Eve's choice through his temptation to have the one thing they weren't supposed to have... fruit from the middle tree. They traded paradise for a taste of the forbidden. It sounds completely stupid, throwing everything away for a momentary selfish pleasure... until we acknowledge that you and I have made that same choice many times over.

So they eat the fruit from the tree of the knowledge of good and evil and innocence was lost. Their immediate reaction is incredibly telling:

> *Then the eyes of both of them were opened, and they knew they were naked; so they sewed fig leaves together and made loincloths for themselves."* – Genesis 3:7 HCSB

Adam and Eve covered their nakedness. They felt shame and made clothes. For the first time there was something between them and God, and between each other too. Later, when God calls out to them, they are hiding in the trees, trembling in fear. God knows exactly what happened, but he makes them say it... *"Who told you that you were naked? Did you eat from the tree I commanded you not to eat from?"*[25] Adam blames Eve, Eve blames the serpent, and fellowship is severed.

This story perfectly illustrates the damage sin does in our lives. It causes a rift in our closeness with God and ushers in things we were never supposed to experience in His presence: shame, embarrassment, guilt, distance. Jesus is the only one who can forgive sin and bring us back where we belong- unbroken fellowship with our Heavenly Father. Without Him no one can know the goodness of paradise ever again.

Adam and Even felt their distance from God, represented in the shame of their nakedness. Children need to feel their distance too. They need to feel naked, exposed, and vulnerable before Him. You've heard it said, "The first step in fixing a problem is understanding you have one." Only when kids realize and acknowledge that they are far from God are they spiritually ready for Jesus to bring them close again. That's true for anyone of any age, really.

So let's get naked and follow Jesus!

Hold on, I'm kidding. Keep your clothes on. Unless you're home alone. Then, you know, whatever floats your boat.

What I really mean is, all people who choose to follow Jesus must first become aware of and acknowledge their need for Him... that's what I mean when I say we must all get naked. Like Adam and Eve, children must realize the cost of their sin and understand that their choices have severed their relationship with God. Only in that place Jesus' work of justification and redemption will make any sense.

> "Like Adam and Eve, children must realize the cost of their sin and undertand that their choices have severed their relationship with God."

Children have to know they have a need. They have to feel the shame of their sin like Adam and Eve. The story is better now than way back in Genesis though. The Apostle Paul tells us we can put on Christ like a garment, be a part of God's family forever, and find paradise again.

> *For as many of you as have been baptized into Christ have put on Christ like a garment. There is no Jew or Greek, slave or free, male or female; for you are all one in Christ Jesus. And if you belong to Christ, then you are Abraham's seed, heirs according to the promise. – Galatians 3:27 HCSB*

WHAT IF I STILL DON'T KNOW?
So you are seeking the Holy Spirit daily for your child and watching for signs that he truly comprehends his great need for Jesus, but you're still unsure if he's ready. He keeps pressing you to take steps toward salvation, but something in your spirit feels uncertain or reluctant. What do you do now?

Here's my best advice:

Relax.

Breathe in. Breathe out.
And slow down.

God is still faithful. He is not the author of confusion and the Holy Spirit is still your guide. In almost every case the right choice is to go slow. The decision to give your life away to Jesus changes everything, and Christ is serious about the level of commitment it takes to walk the narrow road. So if you aren't hearing what you need to hear from your child, keep talking. If you aren't seeing urgency rise in your child, keep watching. If you aren't experiencing comprehension through faith talks keep teaching. It matters enough to take the time to get it right.

There's only one reason I can think of that is not valid for slowing the pace of salvation for your child: fear. Fear that you will mess up, say the wrong things, or mislead your child must be put to bed. That's part of the crippling spirit of defeat I wrote about in chapter one. Salvation is ultimately up to God. He will give you all you need to lead your child successfully. If insecurity about yourself is the thing slowing you down, repent and throw that anxiety away. It's not worth keeping our children from the call on their hearts.

Chapter Wrap Up

The best thing parents can do to gauge the spiritual readiness of children is to draw close to God and trust the leadership of the Holy Spirit. God alone knows the hearts of our kids.

- Salvation starts with God. The only valid reason for a child to choose to follow Jesus is in answer to His call.

- There is no standard age in which children become ready for salvation. God calls each person individually in His timing to respond to the gospel.

- In order to answer God's call, children must understand and acknowledge a deep need inside of themselves.

- Adam and Eve perceived their need for redemption, represented in their shame over being naked. Children must feel this distance too.

Talk About It

The following are questions to answer yourself or talk about in a group.

1. While considering the readiness of your child for the gospel, are you more prone to be hesitant or hurried in your spiritual leadership? What can be the dangers of both approaches?

2. Do your kids love to please you as the parent? If so, how can that complicate their readiness for the gospel?

3. How comfortable are you with telling your children they are "sinners?" Why is it important they understand that concept?

4. How can you help your children realize their need for Jesus?

5. After reading this chapter, what conversations do you need to have with your children to prepare them for the gospel?

WHAT DID I SIGN UP FOR?

Do you remember taking a foreign language in high school? I barely remember my old Latin classes. Someone told me it would help my SAT scores, but studying a dead language really only helped me discover that I don't care anything about Latin. My wife Noël took French in high school and got a lot more out of her language studies than I did… but probably not in the way you think.

One day her French class hosted a guest speaker. His talk must not have been that riveting because Noël doesn't remember a word he said. All she remembers is checking out and whispering with friends around her. At the end of the guest's talk he passed around a sign-up sheet and Noël, without paying a bit of attention to what he said or what the sign-up sheet was for, wrote down her name and phone number. Then she promptly forgot about the whole thing. A short time later Noël's mother received a phone call with some surprising news… her daughter had agreed to host a French foreign exchange student for six weeks.

That's right… Noël accidentally ordered a person from France.

This is not like getting the wrong size shirt in the mail from Amazon; she mistakenly ordered an entire human being. After the shock wore off, her parents decided to honor the commitment and let the French girl come. Her name was Albane and unsurprisingly the whole thing went terribly. Albane didn't like Noël, her friends, or pretty much her entire American experience. The family tried to love her and include her in their church life, vacation, and family time, but she wasn't interested. Eventually Alban went home early without finishing the exchange program.

Obviously Noël had no idea what she was signing up for; she just wrote her name down on a piece of paper. She wasn't prepared or ready for the responsibilities coming her way through a thoughtless, flippant agreement to something she didn't fully understand. The same is true for many people in today's churches. Once, a long time ago for some, they heard someone say they should ask Jesus into their heart. They heard it was the right thing to do, and if they prayed the right words they would go to Heaven. So they said the words, got a pat on the back, and continued on with their lives. The problem is that kind of response doesn't at all vibe with Jesus' words in Luke 9:23:

> Then He said to them all, "If anyone wants to come with Me, he must deny himself, take up his cross daily, and follow Me.[26]

This call is not flippant, and definitely not established on personal benefits. Here in Jesus' words we find cost, surrender, and suffering. It's a total loss of self for the cause of Christ.

Once you recognize as a parent that God is calling your child to Himself, you must remember that the call is not to a prayer, not to a "that sounds good to me so sign me up" kind of decision, but to a **complete life change**. There is so much more to a life of faith than saying a prayer, sitting in a church pew, and then dying and going to Heaven one day. The walk down the narrow road is a journey that must be walked daily, and we must present it that way to our children right from the beginning.

Now, you may be thinking, "Life change is a little much... My kid is a pretty good kid. It's not like he's a drug dealer hanging out on the street corner." You may be right. There are some kids who are born with a sweet disposition and an innate desire to please parents in every way possible. But the spiritual reality is the same for all people, even your "good" children. No matter how well-mannered and respectful your child is, he or she still doesn't reach the standard put forward by Jesus in the Sermon on the Mount when He said, "*Be*

---

26   HCSB

perfect, therefore, as your Heavenly Father is perfect."[27] The best people among us are trapped in death and darkness without Jesus.

I'll never forget what my old Sunday school teacher once told me about this. It was before I had children, but the truth of her words stuck with me long after I became a parent. She was speaking one day about the trouble she was having leading her daughter to follow Christ. Her daughter was raised in a Godly home with parents who led her spiritually and kept her committed to church. Jesus, for her, felt like an entitlement or a birthright. She had grown up singing songs about being Jesus' friend, how He loved her, and about how she loved Him. Why would she need to make some new decision? She couldn't remember a time when she didn't love God.

Here's what that church leader discovered: **sometimes good kids from Godly homes need to get lost before they can get found**. Parents need to help these kids understand that they are utterly hopeless without Christ. Christianity isn't a birthright, it's a personal and active choice that we all must make. It's not crazy to expect our children's entire lives to change. Maybe it's true that your child's behavior doesn't need much modification, but her motivation must move from primarily pleasing you to pleasing God. That's a pretty big transition. Her standards must be driven by the Word of God rather than her own moral compass. That's another big shift. Jesus takes everything old and makes it new… including your well-mannered kid. For that to happen, kids must understand and own their choice for a life of faith.

The first thing we need to explore for leading our kids into salvation in Jesus is the language we use. Their understanding of what God is calling them to will be shaped by the expectations we lay before them in the beginning. Because of this, it's incredibly important to use words that point children to an active response to the Gospel, rather than passive response language.

ACTIVE VS. PASSIVE LANGUAGE
Jesus calls His followers to actively respond to God's call. In His words we find invitations to repentance, life transformation, and active pursuit. He told the fishermen by the edge of the sea to drop their nets and follow Him (Mark 1, Matthew 4). He told the rich young man to sell everything, give to the poor, and then follow Him so that he could have treasure in Heaven (Matthew 19, Mark 10, Luke 18). He told His 12 best friends that unless people loved Him

---

27   Matthew 5:48 HCSB

more than even their parents and children they weren't worthy of Him (Matthew 10). The ending of Luke 9 records some of Jesus' harshest teaching on the cost of following Him:

> *As they were traveling on the road someone said to Him, "I will follow You wherever You go!" Jesus told him, "Foxes have dens, and birds of the sky have nests, but the Son of Man has no place to lay His head." Then He said to another, "Follow Me." "Lord," he said, "first let me go bury my father." But He told him, "Let the dead bury their own dead, but you go and spread the news of the kingdom of God." Another also said, "I will follow You, Lord, but first let me go and say good-bye to those at my house." But Jesus said to him, "No one who puts his hand to the plow and looks back is fit for the kingdom of God."* – Luke 9:57-62 HCSB

You can't read Jesus' words in scripture and not get a sense of the high cost of following Him. He asks in this passage, are you ready to be homeless? Are you willing to drop everything including family affairs? Is there any question or pause in your willingness? If so, you are not ready for this. Now let's contrast what we see in scripture with what we often tell kids who want to make a decision for Christ, "*If you want Jesus to come into your heart, repeat these words after me…*" There is a great gulf between these instructions and the teachings of Jesus. Here's the biggest problem… Words like these don't invite children to actively respond to the Gospel. They are simply repeating words as if they are some kind of magical incantation. Words do not make someone a Christian, it takes a true heart commitment to be a Christ-follower, to take up your cross, to sell everything, to put Jesus first, etc. Remember what we said in chapter three… kids are literal thinkers. If you tell them that saying words will save their souls, they will most likely believe you. Check out this chart that shows the difference between active and passive language:

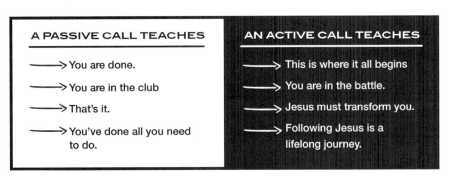

A PASSIVE CALL TEACHES	AN ACTIVE CALL TEACHES
→ You are done.	→ This is where it all begins
→ You are in the club	→ You are in the battle.
→ That's it.	→ Jesus must transform you.
→ You've done all you need to do.	→ Following Jesus is a lifelong journey.

I hope you are starting to see the difference. We must help children understand that the call to faith is a call to action. There's a reason that only a few find life on the narrow road… it's a hard choice. The decision to follow Jesus is not one to be taken lightly. Children aren't just inviting God into their heart, although part of Jesus' free gift of salvation is the indwelling of the Holy Spirit. They are deciding to give their entire life away for the glory of God. That is a lot more of a commitment than simply repeating words in a prayer.

Think about it this way—What's the difference in signing a petition and enlisting into a movement? I've signed plenty of petitions on a variety of important subjects: community projects that should or should not happen, political issues I'm for or against, whether or not I think McDonald's should bring back the McRib, etc. None of those signatures cost me anything. After I signed the paper I continued with my day completely unchanged. Maybe some action occurred that affected me in a small way, but really those actions had nothing to do with my small effort.

> "Words do not make someone a Christian, rather it is a true heart commitment to be a Christ follower, to take up your cross, to sell everything, to put Jesus first."

Compare that to the American civil rights heroes in the 1950's and 60's. Those brave people got on buses, attended rallies, and stood in front of police lines. When they chose to be a part of the movement they were often putting their careers, family life, and even personal safety in jeopardy. Their involvement wasn't just a signature on a piece of paper, it was a total commitment to a cause higher than themselves made with full awareness to the high personal cost required. We know the famous names: Rosa Parks, Medgar Evers, Martin Luther King Jr., James Meredith, etc. There were thousands more who courageously paid high prices for their freedom. Yes, our country still struggles with issues of race, but we are all better today because of their bravery.

When Jesus calls people to repent and follow Him there's a cost, a total surrender to a cause higher than ourselves. This is why our language must invite children to actively give their life away to God, rather than just agree with some truths out of the Bible. When I talk to children about salvation, I rarely say things like, "Ask Jesus into your heart," which doesn't invite children into active lives of faith. I believe phrases that encourage active responses with action verbs to be more effective such as, "Choose to follow Jesus," or "Give your life to Jesus."

Now let's take a moment to breathe. This is pretty heavy stuff, so I need to remind you how great our God is. You can absolutely use all the wrong language with your children and the Holy Spirit can still use your efforts to convince your children to become followers of Jesus. God tends to take our weaknesses and mistakes and turn them into beautiful, reclaimed victories through His grace and mercy. You don't have to be nervous that you will say the wrong things. When you follow God, He turns wrong things into right things. It is still your heart that matters most, and He promises to honor your obedience.

Having said that, as a parent you want to do all you can to get this right. Think about the words you use with your kids. Do you use language that helps them understand that a life of faith means actively following Jesus or do you only talk about the benefits of accepting the free gift of Jesus Christ like Heaven, eternal life, and forgiveness? Don't get me wrong... the free gift of salvation in Jesus is amazing and worth talking about, but we want to be as biblically accurate as possible with our children about the choice they have to make. We do that by using language that is not passive, but rather leads to an active choice for a lifetime of following Jesus.

So What Does My Child Need to Understand About Salvation?

When I talk to a child about following Jesus I keep a mental outline in my head consisting of five major topics to cover: **God's love, sin and consequence, Jesus is the only answer, it's your choice,** and **the free gift**. Let's break down each of those subjects and talk about exactly what kids need to know to grasp the gospel at a young age.

GOD'S LOVE

Kids can't understand anything else about the gospel until they know, believe, and internalize this one huge truth:

God loves me. God loves you.

He loves you... not because of something you did, not because of the language you speak, not because of the way you look, or what you have to offer the world. He just loves you. He knew your name before you were born and the number of hairs on your head[28].

---

28   For me the answer is zero, but probably for you that fact is way more impressive.

For it was You who created my inward parts; You knit me together in my mother's womb. I will praise You because I have been remarkably and wonderfully made. Your works are wonderful, and I know this very well. – Psalm 139:13-14 HCSB

I like to put my hands together and tell children, "God is crazy about you. He wants to be *this close* to you so that He can share His love with you, you can receive His love and love Him back, and for nothing to come between you. Ever!"

If kids can't get this unbelievable, unmatched love God has for them, they'll never understand why Jesus had to go on a rescue mission. It all starts here. God's love starts the most iconic verse in the Bible, *"For God so loved the world..."* [29] And it gives the "why" behind the entire Gospel. Jesus didn't come because we deserved it. He didn't come because we wanted to be saved. He came because God first loved us. That love is the motivator behind everything else that will follow, so it's vital for kids to understand.

SIN & CONSEQUENCES

God loves you and wants to be close to you... Awesome! Sadly, there is a problem with that. You see, although God wants us to stay close to Him and follow His ways, the Bible explains in Romans 3:23 that every single one of us will turn our back on God's way and decide to go our own. Choosing our way over God's way is called **sin**, and it's a serious issue for everyone in the world.

I love to give kids' a simple definition for sin that uses hand motions and helps them identify sin in their own lives: "Sin is anything you THINK (point to your temple), SAY (point to your mouth), or DO (hold out your hands in front of you) that displeases GOD (point up).[30] I love using this particular definition because it allows me to get kids thinking beyond mere actions to the words they use and thoughts they think that aren't pleasing to God. I'll often ask children to give me examples of actions, words, and thoughts that might be a sin and we always have great, clarifying discussions that reveal stuff we all do wrong sometimes. Kids can easily think about things they might have said or done that did not honor God. We need them to connect their own behavior with this spiritual truth.

---

29   John 3:16
30   Again, I think I stole this definition from someone at some convention 100 years ago. I don't remember who, but I've used it ever since. I'll thank you in Heaven.

Now, after reading the last chapter you may be saying, "Wait a minute. Sin is more than just the stuff we do wrong... it's a condition of our heart." I agree, but don't forget... you and I are thinking with grownup brains that can understand abstract concepts. Remember, for children we have to make the abstract concrete. That's why it's easier to talk about personal behavior rather than a condition they inherited from Adam and Eve.

And speaking of abstract, here is where we run into a little trouble with kids. Not only do children need to understand that sin is a problem, they must also understand that there are spiritual consequences for it.

> For the wages of sin is death, but the gift of God is eternal life in Christ Jesus our Lord. – Romans 6:23 HCSB

Death. We earn for death for our sin. How do you think children understand this verse? Kids, thinking without the benefit of a functioning frontal lobe can make two really big mistakes here. They can either think, (a) "Well, I sin and I'm not dead so this stuff must not real," or (b) "I don't want to die! This stuff is really scary!" Neither of those two thoughts lead toward a healthy understanding of spiritual reality without Christ. And so, again we have to find a way to help children understand.

In chapter three I explained that I always try to help kids understand that closeness with God means life and separation from God means death. This is the reason for that. I'm trying to take an abstract, complicated theological truth and make it understandable for children. I make the association that people are made to be close to God and experience life and light in His presence, so that now the consequences of sin actually mean something to a young brain. I tell the child, "When you sin, you are turning your back on God's best for your life. You were made to be close to Him, but when you sin you turn away from Him and separate yourself from His light and life. Remember, closeness with God means life, but being away from God means death." Now (hopefully) I've painted a picture of the ramifications of sin on our spiritual reality and kids can understand what is lost because of it: fellowship, closeness, love relationship, God's presence.

Kids have to get this. God's love is the motivator of the gospel and sin is the great conflict. Following Jesus is just a nice idea without a true understanding of the deep need we all have as guilty sinners. Before our kids can call on a Savior, they have to know they need saving.

JESUS IS THE ONLY ANSWER

Praying every day is a good thing to do. You should go to church as often as you can. Being nice to people, reading your Bible, doing service projects for the community... all great choices.

But none of those things bring you back close to God.

> *Jesus told him, "I am the way, the truth, and the life. No one comes to the Father except through Me." –* John 14:6 HCSB

The only way to find true salvation is to surrender our lives to Jesus. Life starts with this choice. Every other world religion requires effort to please their gods, Christianity requires surrender. Our best efforts are never good enough, that's why we need the grace of Christ. Look at what Paul says about grace in Ephesians 2:8-9:

> *For you are saved by grace through faith, and this is not from yourselves; it is God's gift— not from works, so that no one can boast.*[31]

I am incredibly thankful that my standing with God is not based on how good I can be, but based purely on Jesus' work on my behalf! We have to explain to children that their best effort to please God is not enough. They can't earn their way back to Him, Jesus has to do that for them Himself. To make this point, it is important that children understand the basics of the Biblical gospel narrative so they know exactly what Jesus accomplished. Here's a quick outline:

- God sent His Son Jesus to earth as a baby. He grew up and lived without ever committing a single sin! All He ever did was exactly what His Father wanted Him to do.
- Jesus taught God's ways, healed people, and performed miracles. He got really famous.
- Jesus willingly let Himself get arrested by people who wanted to stop Him from doing the Father's will. They hurt Him really bad and then killed Him by putting Him on a wooden cross. He didn't deserve to die.
- The people put His body in a tomb and sealed it with a big stone. Jesus' body was in there for three whole days.
- On the third day the big rock was rolled away from the opening of the tomb and Jesus was alive again! Hundreds of His friends saw Him and

31   HCSB

talked with Him.

- Now He sits in Heaven on a throne surrounded by angels who praise Him day and night. He will never die again... He is alive forever!

From this true story, children need to grasp three big ideas:

1. Jesus chose to die. We deserve spiritual death because of our sin, but He never sinned.
2. Jesus isn't dead anymore. He'll never die again.
3. When you choose to follow Jesus for yourself, His death counts for you.

These three big ideas are crucial for comprehending the gospel. Children need to know that Jesus chose to die for several reasons. For one, it helps them know that Jesus is altogether different than us. It's one thing to deserve death because of sin (us), and another thing entirely to be perfectly pure and sinless, yet choose punishment and death (Jesus). Children who understand this can see the cross in a brand new light- the ultimate expression of obedience to the Father and love for lost people. Only Jesus could have accomplished the Father's work on the cross. He was no mere man. He was the God-Man.

They also gain a great deal through understanding that Jesus will never die again. There is safety and security in turning your life over to something that is lasting and certain. It gives confidence to a young heart. I don't really think kids can grasp eternity... actually I don't think you or I can grasp the magnitude of forever for that matter. But, in whatever fashion our minds can comprehend, knowing that Jesus is King in Heaven and that's never going to change gives kids a solid foundation to rest their lives upon.

The last big idea is the point we've been trying to set up from the beginning. Jesus' death counts for you if you choose to follow Him. Sin has driven all of us away from life in God's presence, and we deserve death. Jesus died instead. No good work forgives our sin and moves us from death to life, Jesus has to do that for us. He alone took our punishment... He's the only One who could. Through Christ alone we are restored to closeness with God the Father.

IT'S YOUR CHOICE

Here is where active words instead of passive words become so important. Children must understand that they choose to follow Jesus; mom or dad can't make the decision for them. Every single person who desires to come to Jesus must count the cost and determine if he or she is willing to give up everything for the cause of Christ. Even children must realize this is a big, life-altering choice that is not to be taken lightly.

Do you remember the rich young ruler who asked what he could do to receive eternal life? Matthew, Mark, and Luke all record his encounter with Jesus in Judea. In answer to the man's question, Jesus tells him simply to, "… keep the commandments." Of course, that's really not very simple—but our rich friend remained confident. After Jesus lists for him some of the original ten commandments God gave to Moses, the young ruler basically says, "No problem. Done that since birth. Anything else?"[32] Here's Matthew's account of Jesus' answer and the rich young ruler's response.

> *"If you want to be perfect," Jesus said to him, "go, sell your belongings and give to the poor, and you will have treasure in heaven. Then come, follow Me." When the young man heard that command, he went away grieving, because he had many possessions.* – Matthew 19:21-22 HCSB

Jesus drilled down into this guy's heart and found out what he really cared most about: possessions and wealth. It wasn't enough for him to merely *do* things of the faith, in his heart he needed to choose God over every other thing. The rich young ruler left this encounter sad and empty because he just couldn't love God more than everything else in his life.

I tell children often that only one thing can be the king of their hearts. They can't choose Jesus AND anything else. I want them to see their actions, decisions, morality, and values must be governed by the will of Christ alone. Only one thing can be most important in their lives. If it's sports, friends, achievement, or anything else, then Jesus is not in His rightful place. Kids absolutely can be involved in a lot of things, have a lot of friends, and care deeply about their interests, but if any of that stuff is more important than their faith, they will end up sad and empty just like the rich young ruler.

And so kids must choose for themselves whether they are ready to put God first or not. I love the way Jesus illustrates this choice in Matthew 7:13-14. He puts it in plain, concrete imagery that children can easily understand:

> *Enter through the narrow gate. For the gate is wide and the road is broad*

---

32   Obviously this guy wasn't around for the Sermon on the Mount in Matthew 5-7. Jesus said to those in attendance, "Have you been angry? You've committed murder in your heart. Have you looked at a girl with lust in your heart? That's the same as committing adultery." God's standard is simply too high without Jesus… Even for this dude.

that leads to destruction, and there are many who go through it. How narrow is the gate and difficult the road that leads to life, and few find it.[33]

Kids can understand that their lives will be pointed in one of two ways, either toward life following Christ, or towards destruction. You can't go two ways at once. The pathway following Christ isn't easy... most people do not choose it. But it's the only path that leads toward life, so it's worth it for those truly willing to call Jesus the King of their hearts.

There's a theological term for turning from one way and going another— **repentance**. It's an incredibly important topic that most children never hear about. Repentance is not really a word you hear on the playground or on the Disney Channel, but that doesn't make it any less relevant. When I teach the term to children I tell them that repentance is made up of three active decisions:

1. **Stop**—Your life is headed the wrong way. You are making choices based on what you want and what you think is best. You must decide today to stop going your own way down the broad road that leads to destruction.
2. **Turn**—you must turn away from the things you used to care about the most and turn to Christ. Make Him the One thing you look to as King of your heart.
3. **Go a New Direction**—Decide today you want to follow Jesus, give your life to Him, and live how He wants you to live.

Many times I will actually demonstrate the three components of repentance with my body by walking one way, stopping, turning around, and walking a new direction. When demonstrated visually, repentance is very easy to get for kids, and it's crucial for the right understanding of the Gospel. The New Testament is full of calls by Jesus and the leaders of the first church to repent. Here are a few:

From then on Jesus began to preach, "Repent, because the kingdom of heaven has come near!" – Matthew 4:17 HCSB

Jesus replied to them, "The healthy don't need a doctor, but the sick do. I have not come to call the righteous, but sinners to repentance." – Luke 5:31-32 HCSB

---

33   HCSB

"Repent," Peter said to them, "and be baptized, each of you, in the name of Jesus Christ for the forgiveness of your sins, and you will receive the gift of the Holy Spirit." – Acts 2:38 HCSB

And now, brothers, I know that you did it in ignorance, just as your leaders also did. But what God predicted through the mouth of all the prophets—that His Messiah would suffer—He has fulfilled in this way. Therefore repent and turn back, so that your sins may be wiped out, that seasons of refreshing may come from the presence of the Lord. – Acts 3:17-19 HCSB

Ultimately of course, it's up to you how you teach your children the importance of choosing Christ for themselves above everything else. Again, we don't want to paint a picture using passive language and have our children believe they can say some words and receive salvation. This is an active choice that will change the course of their entire lives. That means we, as spiritual leaders to our kids, have a responsibility to help them understand the importance of making this decision for themselves.

THE FREE GIFT

The second part of Romans 6:23 tells us about the best gift we will ever receive. It's better than the coolest gadget and the most expensive toy.... And here's the best part: God gives it to everyone who chooses to follow His Son, Jesus.

For the wages of sin is death, but the gift of God is eternal life in Christ Jesus our Lord.[34]

Now, I purposefully haven't keyed on the free gift yet. I believe the Gospel is more about God's love and our need for restoration that only comes through Jesus. Often, when we begin with all the benefits of following Jesus, we present salvation as a means to collecting eternal rewards that serve us... Of course followers of Christ benefit from undeserved blessings, but following Jesus is really about glorifying God and not ourselves.

That being said, there are incredible blessings within God's free gift that are essential for a child to understand. When I talk to kids about the free gift I break it down into six components. There are many more privileges for the adopted children of God, but these are a great starting place:

---

34   HCSB

1. Forgiveness—When Jesus took our punishment on the cross He purified us from every sin we will ever commit. The Bible says, "As far as the east is from the west, so far has He removed our transgressions from us,"[35] and He, "will never again remember (our) sins."[36] Forgiveness through Jesus is absolutely complete for all our guilt today and even all our sins in the future.

2. Heaven—Followers of Jesus get to live in Heaven with Jesus after our life on earth is over. No, we don't become angels strumming harps on little clouds... First of all, people don't become angels, angels are angels. Secondly, Heaven is way better than that. The Bible tells us there are streets of pure gold like transparent glass and 12 gates at the entrance, each made of a single pearl.[37] It also says that Jesus has prepared mansions for His followers behind those gates where we will live without tears or pain or sickness or death.[38] Best of all Jesus is there. Bible says we will see His face and there will be no more night. We will celebrate Him without ceasing and He will reign forever![39]

3. Eternal Life- One day our bodies will die. This is true for everyone, but that doesn't mean it's the end though. The souls of every follower of Jesus will live on in a new, better, complete body that will never die. There will be no more sickness or death or sadness... only joy in the presence of God forever.

4. The Holy Spirit Inside- In Paul's first letter to the Corinthians he asks them, "Don't you know that your body is a sanctuary of the Holy Spirit who is in you, whom you have from God?"[40] Although the word "indwelling" is a little tough for kids to understand, this is an important part of the free gift of God to know about. The Holy Spirit is our helper.[41] The Bible says that He prays for us when we don't know what to pray.[42] He is our guide, helping us make decisions that honor God and governing our minds.[43] He helps us understand scripture,[44] teaches us God's truth,[45] helps us witness for God,[46] and convicts our hearts when we do wrong. The Holy Spirit is a full

---

35	Psalm 103:12
36	Hebrews 8:12
37	Revelation 21:21
38	John 14:2, Revelation 21:4
39	Revelation 22:1-5
40	1 Corinthians 6:19
41	John 14:26
42	Romans 8:26
43	Luke 12:12
44	1 Corinthians 2:14
45	1 John 2:27
46	1 John 4:2-3

member of the Trinity and His presence is gifted to all who follow the Son. Mercy- These next two parts of Jesus' free gift are a little tricky because they are so similar. Mercy can be described as NOT getting what we deserve. Because of sin all people deserve death, separation from God, punishment, and darkness. Through the free gift of Jesus Christ we don't have to experience any one of those things. God gives us great relief through His wonderful mercy.

5. Grace- Likewise, grace is GETTING what we DON'T deserve. We don't deserve favor with God. We don't deserve to be called sons and daughters through holy adoption. We don't deserve kindness or blessings or our every need met according to our Father's riches in Heaven. But through amazing grace, God pours all of these out on us in full measure.

As you can see, the free gift of God through Jesus is an extravagant, amazing blessing for all who choose to receive it. Although I've focused mainly on the

sacrificial love of the father as expressed through Jesus, it is a sweet and overwhelming benefit of walking the narrow road.

GETTING TO THE POINT

Once you've determined that your child understands the gospel and sensed a calling from God to follow Jesus, there's nothing stopping you from helping your child surrender his life to God. Sometimes parents are a bit intimidated to take on this moment and lead, afraid they are going to get something wrong. Remember, the words of a prayer don't save people. It's not the **words**, it's the **decision**.

So breathe in, breathe out... relax. You can do this. Share this wonderful news with your family. Whisper about God's love in your infant's ear. Every now and then decide to forgive a punishment your first grader rightfully deserves and use the occasion to explain the beautiful free gift of mercy and grace. Remind your entire family on the car ride to church that attending a Sunday morning service is a great thing, but everyone in the car one day must make a decision for themselves whether or not to give their lives to Jesus and you can't do that for them. Pepper your conversations with gospel teachings until your children are ready to make a decision for Christ, and then keep the conversation going even after. The Good News of Jesus is the most important thing your children will ever hear, and they need to hear it from you.[47]

47   Although the heart is much more important than the words for the moment of salva-

One last subject before we close this chapter out: If your child does make a decision to follow Jesus, be sure to let the children's pastor know at your church. Once the choice is made, children need to mark the occasion and make the decision public by getting baptized. Baptism is a special opportunity to celebrate a major milestone in a child's life. I tell kids there are three great reasons to participate in water baptism:

1. **The Bible tells us to do it.** Jesus was baptized Himself and then commanded His followers to go make disciples in every nation and baptize them in the name if the Father, Son, and Holy Spirit.[48] That alone is reason enough.

2. **It's a *public profession* of our faith.** To help kids understand what this means, I explain that baptism is a lot like wearing a jersey on a sport's team. If I look out on a playing field and I see athletes wearing a certain color, I automatically know what team they are on. The same is true for baptism… it shows the whole world that you are on God's team through Jesus.

3. **It shows a picture of what Jesus has done in our hearts.** The act of baptism itself is highly symbolic. In the water we can see the death, burial, and resurrection of Jesus, the washing away of sins, and our old selves being buried with Christ and then raised to, "walk in a new way of life."[49] This symbolism can be tough for a child to understand, so we have to be careful here. The main goal is to help them comprehend that the act doesn't accomplish these things (washing of sins, new life, etc), rather it *symbolizes* these things.

On the occasion of your child's baptism you have one job as a parent… celebrate as hard you possibly can! You want your child to remember this day for the rest of her life, and allow baptism to be a spiritual anchor she can always remember. A lot of things will transpire over the course of her life. She will go through many ups and downs. Give her a strong memory of the day she obeyed and showed the world her faith in Jesus and it will serve to bring her back to her identity as a Christ-follower again and again.

---

tion, I realize some parents might appreciate a little more help leading a child through making this decision. For a little more coaching on this, check out appendix three at the end of this book, The ABCs of Salvation.
48   Matthew 28:18-20
49   Romans 6:4

Chapter Wrap Up

- When a child is ready to follow Jesus, parents must help him understand he is not merely saying words in a prayer. Instead, he is committing to a complete life-change.

- Language that invites children to actively respond to the gospel gives them accurate understanding of their responsibility to live a life of faith.

- Passive-response language misrepresents the commitment needed to follow Jesus and should be avoided.

- Children should understand five major topics in order to make a well-informed decision for Christ: God's Love, Sin and Consequences, Jesus is the Only Answer, It's Your Choice, and the Free Gift.

- Repentance is made up of three active decisions children must make: stop, turn, and go a new direction.

- Baptism is a special opportunity to celebrate a major milestone in a child's life.

Talk About It

The following are questions to answer yourself or talk about in a group.

1. In your own words explain the difference between active and passive language when leading kids to respond to the gospel call.

2. Why is active response language so important?

3. Are you comfortable sharing the gospel message with your children? Which of the 5 topics (God's love, sin and consequence, Jesus is the only answer, it's your choice, and the free gift) do you feel the least equipped to talk about and what will you do about it?

4. Why is it so important to emphasize with children that they must choose to follow Jesus for themselves?

5. Which of the five salvation topics do you think you need to start today talking to your kids about?

PART THREE

THE FAMILY OF FAITH

7

COUNTERCULTURAL FAMILIES

A few years back I came up with a startling realization in my family. If I prayed for God to make my kids different, and I taught them Christian values different than the world's values, and if we made decisions based on a different set of beliefs…

…Then there was a strong possibility that my kids would end up different than other kids. Shocking, I know.

My kids are different kids. My oldest two have made decisions to follow Jesus, and we are praying for the day He calls my other two little ones into relationship with Him through Jesus. Because we choose as a family to live differently, they don't always get the cultural references their classmates talk about. They don't see some of the current movies or hear the most popular music. They don't know what is happening on Snapchat or see every meme that blows up. Sometimes they are left out of conversations because of the choices we've made together. Walking the narrow road isn't easy for anyone at any age.

Every now and then a little lie will creep into my brain. I will believe for a moment that I am messing up my children and making their lives miserable. The fact that my family is countercultural makes some of their friendships difficult, especially in the crucible of upper elementary and junior high. If I was a better father I would help my children relate by introducing them to whatever R-rated reference the other kids are talking about, the lie goes. If I really cared about my children, I would let them go to every sleepover and every party regardless of the environment inside the hosting home. That would help them, I hear whispered in my ear. That would make their lives better.

Of course this is stupid, backwards logic from the pit of hell. Jesus calls His followers to be different from the world. It's a good thing to be countercultural, but that doesn't mean it's easy. No one really wants to be an outcast, young or old. I do desire for my children to have friends (and thankfully they do), but popularity isn't our highest family priority. Our main goal is to follow Christ and make decisions that glorify God. However, from time to time pressure comes along to push us back from radically following Christ and move toward conformity. It's important when those times come to recognize those pressures and reevaluate the motivations behind each family choice.

PEER PRESSURE

I think I naively believed when I was younger peer pressure would disappear when I reached a certain age. I thought adults didn't worry with the expectations of others once they got old enough to identify it. Boy, was I wrong. I've watched parents make decisions, not because it was what they wanted or thought was right, but because they believed they had no choice. Some parents don't believe they can say no when a coach schedules practices on Sunday morning. Others spend money they don't have to make sure their children wear the right shoes. Still others involve their children in activities every night of the week because other parents do it for their kids. All of this happens, not because we are focused on what is best for our kids, but because we focus on what families are doing around us.

Kristen Welch, in her great book *Raising Grateful Kids in an Entitled World*, shares a story that perfectly illustrates how easily pressure from other parents can slip in and affect us without warning. She writes that after moving to a new town and joining a moms' Bible study to make friends, she sat at a table and listened to other moms talk about the importance of their kids getting in the best preschools. I'll let her tell the rest:

> *"They talked about waiting lists and registration fees and monthly tuition. I didn't say a word—I just listened. By the end of the class my stomach was*

in a knot.

Worry about preschool? I didn't know it was something I needed to do. It was the first time I can remember feeling like I owed my children something I couldn't provide. And it was a terrible feeling. I loved my kids as much as my new friends did theirs, and it seemed if everyone else said preschool was a priority, I should make it one too. Even though it sounds immature and naïve, that's how I spent my early parenting years—trying to give my kids everything because everyone else was."[50]

Peer pressure can negatively affect family life in several ways: it can make you feel lousy about your own family, push you to reach for an unattainable pace of life, live beyond your financial means, or cause you to undermine your values in order to fit in. It sneaks into parenting through seemingly positive, loving thoughts:

- I want to give my children everything other kids have.

- I need to do everything I can now to help my children reach their full potential, no matter the cost.

- I don't want my kids to feel left out.

- I want my child to be happy.

These good thoughts (and others like them) unchecked by a biblical world-view can easily lead you places you never wanted to go. As an example, let's take the idea that as a parent your job is to help your child reach his or her fullest potential no matter the cost. Say you sign up your daughter to play softball in the local rec league. She shows promise in the infield and soon gets recruited to play on a tournament squad. Now, this tournament squad practices three nights a week and travels to play other talented teams all across the state. You're not sure you have the time or the resources to be a part of this program, but the coach assures you the only way for your daughter to stay competitive with other girls her age is to continually play against the best talent. And actually, your daughter isn't quite experienced enough yet to make the starting lineup, so it's in her best interest to hire a hitting coach for extra batting practice on your off nights. After all, it's what all the other parents

---

50   Kristen Welch, Raising Grateful Kids in an Entitled World: How One Family Learned That Saying No Can Lead to Life's Biggest Yes (Carol Stream, Illinois: Tyndale), 46.

are doing for their girls. All of the sudden, a fun extracurricular activity has turned into a huge financial and scheduling burden... you don't want to be the reason your daughter doesn't become the next star of the softball diamond.

Now, maybe your family loves spending every free minute on the ball field, maybe you don't... either way, it's unhealthy to make decisions based upon what people around you are doing. What others do has absolutely no bearing on God's best for you. Comparing is a road that only leads away from His plans for your family.

Honestly we can blame Facebook and Instagram for some of this tension (or whatever social media platform is popular when you are reading this book). At any point in time we can go online and see smiling pictures of our friends doing something awesome. It's easy to think, "The Smiths took their kids to the park and had the best time after school today. All we did was come home and eat leftover lasagna. I'm an awful parent." This is the harm in measuring your life against others. You know what we don't see? Thirty seconds after that picture went online one Smith child pushed the other Smith child down, made him cry, and everyone went home from the park angry... parents included. That stuff doesn't tend to make it online. Usually it's only smiling, happy faces that paint a false sense of reality for those of us scrolling through our newsfeed. We see it, we compare, and we feel the pressure of not measuring up. It's another tool of our spiritual enemy to beat us down and introduce the spirit of defeat into our home leadership.

Sadly, I've even seen peer pressure negatively impact families inside the church. Just because a mom or dad sits in the same worship service as you, doesn't mean they share your values. Parents tend to lower their principles to fit the group they attach themselves to, instead of reaching together for the highest standards achievable. Rather than be viewed as *radical*, some church families want to be viewed as *normal* or *down to earth*. And so great Christian people make concessions they never intended to make because other great Christian people in their life do the same thing. The check in their spirit for parental decisions is overcome by the desire to belong in their heart.

"The only reason to do anything is because it is the best way for your family to glorify God right now."

Look, peer pressure is real. If we don't recognize it for what it is, we will make family decisions for the wrong reasons. Really, the only reason to do anything is because it's the best way for your family to glorify God right now. Your journey down the narrow road has nothing to do with anyone else's choices and decisions. I'm a broken record by now... your best bet is to draw close to God through scripture and prayer and let what He starts in your heart flow down into your children's lives. Getting your clues from the families around you just doesn't work.

KID PRESSURE

It stinks to say no to our children, doesn't it? I hate disappointing my kids... I really do. The accommodating part of me wants to give and give and fill my house with laughter and joy. The selfish part of me wants my kids to think I'm the cool dad who is free and generous with the word "yes."

But that's not what's best for them. And I can't expect them to understand that.

My oldest daughter Sophie hates eating food. You heard me... all food.[51] Honestly, I don't know how she is still alive. If she had her way she would eat chicken nuggets, macaroni and cheese, and possibly some yogurt for every meal for the rest of her life. And even then it would have to be the *right* chicken nuggets, the *one kind* of mac and cheese she likes, and don't even try that Greek yogurt grossness. My wife does an awesome job of forcing... ahem, I mean *encouraging*... her to eat whatever is on her plate for the meal, but the results are battle after battle at dinnertime. Honestly, it would be so much easier to give up. I prefer harmony at the table where laughter and conversation flow and no one cries over green beans. But that's just not going to happen at my house on many nights for a couple of reasons: First, Sophie needs nutrition. It's not in her best interest to eat only the food she enjoys. If we gave in to her constant resistance her body would not grow and develop and flourish physically the way it's supposed to. Secondly, Sophie doesn't get to make the rules in my house. That's not her place in the family. Her place is to be a kid and follow the rules. If that gets out of order I have not fulfilled my Biblical calling to lead my family. I've also given her a wrong picture of what it means to respect authority and submit to headship in her life. This is no small issue. If she doesn't learn obedience to mom and dad right now, it's highly likely she will struggle with all authority in her life: teachers, bosses, and the Highest Authority— God. And so Sophie's got to eat those dumb beans on

---

51   Well, maybe it just seems that way.

her plate if it kills us all.

There are a few things that most kids just know.[52] One thing they understand pretty clearly is that discipline is a pain in the neck for parents. Usually punishment for kids is punishment for parents too. Take away a teen's car for a week and suddenly mom and dad find their chauffeur duties increased significantly. Restrict a child from TV and now the TV is off for the entire family. Time out chairs for little ones mean the possibility of moaning and complaining and drama for much longer than the actual punishment lasts. Kids know these things and manipulate their reactions in hopes that parents toss up their hands and say, "It's not worth it, here are your stupid keys," or whatever. As I've heard it said, "We ain't raisin' no dummies."

Kids also know just how to pull heart-strings to get what they want. If a child has two parents (married or divorced), she knows just how to appeal to whichever parent she is talking to, and if that doesn't work, play both parents against each other. You know this trick because you pulled it when you were a kid. Here's how it goes:

- A little girl who wants something will ask Mom. Mom says no.
- The little girl then seeks out daddy, serves him his favorite beverage, curls up in his lap, and tells him how much she loves him. She then sweetly asks for the thing again. Dad says yes.
- The little girl gets the thing. Mom sees her with the thing and gets angry.
- Mom says, "I thought I told you NO!" Little girl answers, "Daddy said yes."
- Mom gets angry with Dad and tells him she should have married her high school sweetheart who is now a successful neurosurgeon. Dad wonders what in the world just happened.

Poor Dad. He never saw his little con artist coming. More than likely mom had a good reason for saying no the first time, but the little girl wanted what she wanted and used manipulation to get her way. The easy response here is to just let it go, let the daughter have the thing already, and just be done with it—especially if this episode went down in the midst of a busy schedule. Of course, if that's the choice you make, our little manipulator has suddenly discovered a nifty tool for getting every single thing she wants in life. I wonder if she'll ever try this again?

---

52   I suspect babies are given tiny little books at birth with titles like Tried and True Methods for Getting Your Way Every Time and The Public Tantrum: Embarrassing for Them, Effective for You! I don't know where those tiny, little fingers are hiding them though.

We shouldn't be surprised when kids put pressure on parents to get their way in the home... part of being a broken, sinful human being is desiring selfish gains. We can't, however, let that pressure break us into submission to our children's will. There's nothing wrong with wanting your children to be happy, but happiness is not the highest goal. We want our families to be *different*. Sometimes that means saying no and disappointing our children. Sometimes that means resisting their desires and denying them something they want. Sometimes that means making choices other families won't make and causing life to be difficult for teens petrified of sticking out in the crowd. The immediate battles may be fierce, but in the long run our children need lessons and convictions taught by uncompromised commitment to Christian values.

It's hard but it's worth it.

COUNTERCULTURE FAMILIES

So, you're ready for your family to commit to the narrow road together, no matter what pressure may come. What does that look like? Honestly it looks like tough choices made every single day. Although we will get into some deeper level practices of faith in this section, I still maintain there is no substitute for drawing close to God and letting faith flow down into family life. When a parent commits to living out the Shema, countercultural decisions are the natural result. The Holy Spirit guides us away from worldly thoughts and practices and leads toward God's best for our lives.

But now let's add some intention to it. Let's get beyond the incredibly important practice of weighing each moment as it comes and applying faith to every decision and reaction, to making purposeful strides toward countercultural parenting. I would suggest three steps to ensure your family lives differently than the world:

1. TALK ABOUT IT
When I call a family meeting my kids usually assume something bad is coming. It's true... sometimes I share sad or disappointing news in this setting (like a move or a death in the family), but sometimes we just need to do some business. The decision to live as a counterculture family will affect everyone in your household, so a group conversation is a good idea. Yes, your kids may freak out a little if they aren't used to having family meetings, but just imagine how relieved they'll be when no one is in trouble!

Sit everyone down and talk about what you want to do. Tell your kids that you desire to live differently than the rest of the world. Let them know as a family you want to make the things of God your highest priority. Explain that you plan on making choices based on God's truth in scripture and it may require missing out on certain things, not taking part in certain activities, or going without some things. Remind the children that your highest goal is to glorify God, and that living for Him is far better than anything worldly that would detract from His best for your family. Ask them to partner with you in living differently. Bring them into the conversation and show them you are serious about the decision and respect them as full members of the family.

2. COMMIT TO YOUR LOCAL CHURCH

I know this seems so obvious, but real commitment to Biblical community is rare these days. I'm not talking about coming once a month… that's convenience, not commitment. I'm talking about sold out, unwavering passion to take your place in the Bride of Christ—God's people.

When I was in college my friends and I had long conversations about what was wrong with American churches. In truth I could count the number of churches I actually had personal knowledge about on one hand. Now that I've been blessed to interact with faith communities all across the country, I can truly say I've found inspiring Christ followers in every single one. Are there messes in some of these churches? Sure. But are all these churches extensions of Christ's mission to the world? I've seen beautiful examples of sacrifice, service, and love more times than I can count. And I grew really tired of talking about what is wrong with Christians when so many things are right.

I know some are skeptical about the politics and hypocrisy found in many churches… I get it. Honestly, we've earned a lot of the criticisms. It absolutely breaks my heart to think about the ones who've been hurt by the very people charged in scripture to be the embodiment of Jesus' love and grace to the world. But even this reality doesn't negate the command spoken by Jesus in John 13:

> *"I give you a new command: Love one another. Just as I have loved you, you must also love one another. By this all people will know that you are My disciples, if you have love for one another."* – John 13:34-35 HCSB

Countercultural families are deeply committed to the local church. They don't just attend, they immerse fully into the mission and vision of their community of faith and actively love their brothers and sisters in Christ. This means modeling for your kids what it means to fellowship and study the Bible with other believers in a small group environment. It means tithing. It means praying for your pastor and other leaders in the church. It also means finding a place of service within the church and using your gifts and talents to help do your part. Even your older kids can serve in some capacity. Teaching them to come and give is so much better than teaching them to come and receive, and it helps them formulate a right attitude about their responsibilities to the church now and in the future. In my experience it's rare for a kid not to "get it" even after a short time serving the church. I asked my son the other day which he would give up if I forced him to: his eighth grade boys small group with his buddies or serving in the two-year-old class on Sunday mornings. He didn't hesitate for a second before choosing to stay with the preschoolers.

3. SERVE PEOPLE CLOSE BY AND AROUND THE WORLD

There is just something powerful about serving people. Recently some friends talked my wife and me into serving a local inner-city ministry that does street evangelism, ministry to assisted living facilities, and other projects on Friday nights. It was a great time, we worked with our friends, and then it was over … or so I thought. My wife decided we needed to bring our children back for the experience as soon as we could. Now, one Friday night is okay, but come on … another one? It's *Friday night* for crying out loud. Can't we find a place that does projects on Saturday from 9am to 10am? Serving on Friday isn't very convenient for my "me-time" schedule. My mouth said, "great idea," but my heart said, "aw, man."

As soon as I saw my children caring for other people, helping to serve food, and speaking to new folks with kindness my heart changed. This always happens. Every time we serve together as a family I'm reminded how important it is and how much we all love giving to others. All reluctance in my heart gets buried under the weight of joy in seeing my kids serve. Every. Single. Time.

The average family doesn't spend Friday nights or Saturday mornings or any other time serving their community. Even fewer families choose to use vacation for short term mission trips a few hours away from home. Still fewer spend hard-earned money to fly to an impoverished country to serve people who speak other languages. What kind of family are you going to be? This is countercultural activity for people willing to risk and live differently. Serving doesn't have to organized by a ministry or mission organization, either. You can work together to cut an elderly person's grass. You can rake the leaves in front of the local elementary school and haul them away. You can play a game in which each of you races to find 8 things in your closet to donate to a local women's shelter. The point is to serve as a family and reinforce selfless values that help you obey Jesus' teaching in Matthew 22:39: "Love your neighbor as yourself."

I'll end this chapter by asking the question again…

What kind of family do you want to be?

Honestly it's hard to stick out and operate outside of cultural norms. I'd say it's harder for the children, but that would be a lie. It's hard for everyone. But the fact remains… we can either walk the narrow road that leads to life, or we can choose the path of normalcy. You only get to select one road. If we choose the narrow road it will probably alienate us from people who don't understand truly surrendered living, but thankfully we won't walk alone. We will have the greatest love the universe has ever known to accompany us all the way.

> *Look at how great a love the Father has given us that we should be called God's children. And we are! The reason the world does not know us is that it didn't know Him.* – 1 John 3:1 HCSB

Chapter Wrap Up

- Although difficult, Christian families are called to be different from other families with different values and beliefs.

- Peer pressure exists among parents, but the only reason to do anything is because it's the best way for your family to glorify God right now.

- The happiness of children is not the highest goal of the home. Honoring God as a family sometimes means saying no and disappointing your kids.

- Countercultural families are deeply committed to the local church.

- Countercultural families lead a life of service together.

Talk About It

The following are questions to answer yourself or talk about in a group.

1. In what ways have you experienced both positive and negative peer pressure in parenting? How do you go about overcoming the negative pressure from families around you?

2. When have you enforced rules with your children even though it would have been much easier to simply let it go? Was it worth it?

3. Would you call your family a countercultural family? If so, how are you different than the world?

4. Would you say you've taught your children to value the local church through your commitment to it? In what ways do you need to show your family that church is a priority?

5. Have you ever served your community or taken part in a mission project with your kids? If not, how can service become a part of your family's spiritual life?

8

BE THE PARENT

Two of my children are incredibly strong-willed.[53] I absolutely love the independence, strength of character, and leadership qualities that come along with this trait. From experience I can tell you it is so cool to see these kids turn into exceptional young people who chase after what they believe in with determination and unyielding resolve.

But getting them there can be... how do I put this?

Challenging.

Early in parenting life my wife and I were absolutely at our end with one of our strong-willed kids. I can remember driving from Hattiesburg, Mississippi to Montgomery, Alabama in a little car with our toddler buckled in the back.[54] About every 45 seconds he would scream as loud as he possibly could, not because he was hungry or sleepy or needed a diaper change, he was just bored. Every scream felt like an ice pick getting jammed into my eardrum over and over and over and over again. For five hours. We fussed at him, pulled over and spanked him, threatened him, turned up the music on the

---

53   I need to pause here and say a quick thank you to Dr. James Dobson for his exceptionally great book The Strong-Willed Child. Count the Hales among the many, many families this resource has helped.
54   Trust me, there is no good way to get from Hattiesburg to Montgomery in a car. Winding, two-lane roads are your only option. It takes for-ev-er.

radio to ignore him, but nothing worked. In fact, I think our slow slide into insanity actually gave my little guy some pleasure, like a game to see which parent would be the first to yell, "I can't take it anymore!" and fling ourselves from the moving car. There were some irrational moments on that trip when we really thought, "We can't raise this kid. We're going to have to leave him in Alabama."

Don't judge us. We didn't actually do it.

I can remember in those early years thinking we were the worst parents on the planet. The constant struggle with my strong-willed kid was exhausting and defeating, especially for Noël who stayed home with him during the day. The peace and joy I longed for in my family was nonexistent and I didn't have an answer to fix it... until one pivotal day that changed everything. Yes, we still struggled sometimes, and yes my son was still a challenge to raise, but our perspective completely shifted on this day for the better. Let me tell you what happened:

I came home from work to find my wife and son engaged in an all-out war. He had done something (I can't remember what) and needed to be disciplined. Noël was doing all she could just to get him into his room for a punishment, but he fought her with all of his strength. He pushed away, grabbed onto door frames, screamed, went limp—every single trick in the book. Noël was incredibly frustrated, so she engaged right back arguing and struggling and straining to get him in that room. Now, this could just have easily been me. I raised my voice and went toe-to-toe with my son in plenty of battles. But for the first time on that day I saw clearly what was happening in the moment:

We were lowering ourselves to his level.

I remember thinking, "In this argument, they sound like peers. We are not his peers, we are his parents." And so I decided to take a big risk. First, I removed Noël from the situation so she could cool down a little bit. Then I went calmly to my son and said, "You disobeyed your mom, and now you need a spanking. I will be in your room." Then I simply walked into his room, sat down in a chair, and waited. All my cards were on the table. I didn't try to pick him up, I didn't yell to convince him to come inside, I just sat and prayed for this new tactic to work.

It only took a moment for my son to peek into the room, shuffle over to my chair, and crawl into my lap. We talked about what he had done, I delivered the punishment, and then hugged him and told him I loved him very much and always would no matter what. Just like that it was over.

Ever since that day Noël and I have held a new mantra: *Be the parent.* This statement means a lot in our house. It reminds us not to sink to our kids' level, but to lead them with the authority granted us as heads of the house. It encourages us to step into the hard stuff of life, even when it's uncomfortable. It

> "Being the parent is not easy, but no one else can do it. It's on us to rise to our position and meet the challenge head-on."

means we tell the kids the truth about everything, because there are some things they need to hear from us and not their friends. Being the parent is not easy, but no one else can do it. It's on us to rise to our position and meet the challenge head-on.

The following are some things you can do to be the parent in your home:

SET BOUNDARIES

Parents set boundaries and kids push against them. It's always been that way and will continue to be that way until Jesus comes back. In fact, it's a good thing as your child matures into adolescence for her to push for more autonomy and independence. It's part of preparing for adulthood. But here's something really important most kids don't know about themselves and most parents forget as they lose perspective in the grind of raising kids: they aren't pushing against boundaries because they don't want them, they're pushing to make sure these boundaries are strong enough to protect them. Kids want boundaries, whether they know it or not. Dr. James Dobson talks about the safety children feel with clear, communicated limits:

> "There is security in defined limits. When the home atmosphere is as it should be, children live in utter safety. They never get in trouble unless they deliberately ask for it, and as long as they stay within the limits, there is happiness and freedom and acceptance."[55]

Beyond safety and happiness, setting up boundaries lets kids know that parents are taking their rightful roles as their allies and leaders. According to

---

55   James Dobson, "Do Kids Really Want Boundaries," drjamesdobson.org.

Betsy Hart, author of *It Takes a Parent,* boundaries tell our kids, "I'm on your side."

> "Most parents have figured out that it's great to be on their child's side, but the way many parents get there is backward. In our culture, 'I'm on your side' has come to mean, 'I'll give to you, or do for you, or give in to you—whatever you want. Just please accept me. Please acknowledge me. Please like me. Please be nice to me. Please *let* me be on your side.'
>
> When I say, 'I'm on your side,' I'm talking about just the opposite of such an approach. I'm talking about a parent who is willing to wrestle with his child for the heart of that child, as if that child's very life and soul are at stake. Because they are."[56]

Of course, once you set boundaries, you have to keep them. If you don't, they aren't really boundaries in the first place. Your kids will find the weak place in your wall of protection and push until it crumbles, so you have to be ready to consistently enforce the boundaries you set up. In this endeavor you've simply got to be the parent. Do the hard work now and you can keep your credibility as leader of the family later. Then, once you are ready to speak life in to your children and let God's work in you flow down to your family, your children can trust you mean what you say.

ANSWER THE QUESTIONS

My pastor friend, Steve Parten, gave me some excellent advice several years ago—never be shocked or embarrassed by anything my children ask. Answer every question plainly, and if I have to blush or faint or freak out, do it in another room away from the kids. His point was that I must take every measure possible to be a safe place for my kids. If I avoid a question or act uncomfortable, I am expressing with my actions they should go elsewhere for sensitive information. I've got to be the parent in this situation... sending my kids in another direction to find out important stuff is the last thing I want to happen.

I don't know who decided talking about puberty and sex should be saved for one giant, awkward conversation. It certainly doesn't match the strategy of allowing faith to flow down in the natural context of daily life. I don't want to have the "birds and the bees" talk with my kids. Instead, I want to have

---

56   Betsy Hart, It Takes a Parent (New York: G.P. Putnam's Sons, 2005), 47.

several conversations as they come up and answer every question they ask. And believe me it comes up in my house.

The other day one of my children learned about a certain sexual act at school he hadn't heard of before. In the car later that day he asked me what it was, and so I told him using plain language as matter-of-factly as I could. I then took the opportunity to tell him again that God made sex for married people to enjoy, and what might sound weird to him now might flow naturally one day when he finds freedom and pleasure in expressing his love to his future wife. Then he asked me if Noël and I had ever tried it! For as many tough conversations as I've had with my kids, I admit I almost bowed out this one, turned up the radio, and pretended that I didn't hear him. Instead I took a deep breath and asked, "Do you really want to know?"[57]

I absolutely love that my son feels safe enough with me to ask me really personal questions. If he had settled for whatever information he'd heard at school, no doubt he would have been confused at best and misinformed at worst. His buddies who think they know about sex don't know anything at all, but I can take that moment to let faith flow down through teaching about sex in the right context of marriage.

If you want to know, I started talking to my boys about sex around first grade. At that stage they couldn't possibly understand the emotional connection, desire, and intimacy of it. All they could really understand is the mechanics and directive to first be married. We talked about boy parts, girl parts, eggs, sperm, and how God designs bodies to fit together. We also talked a little bit about some of the negative consequences of sex outside of marriage. As they grew older our conversation widened to puberty, body changes, and other important maturity topics long before the boys actually experienced them. Honestly, this stuff was pretty easy to talk about. It wasn't weird because I didn't make it weird. I just answered questions and let faith flow down. Now my girls are growing up and it's time for Noël to take the lead on this journey. Check back with me in 15 years and I'll tell you how it went.

Of course, sex isn't the only difficult topic we've got to engage in to be the parent. What if your son says one day, "I've been thinking about it, and I don't think I believe in God anymore," or your teen asks, "How do you know the Bible is true? I've read some things that make me wonder," or, your youngest daughter says, "Why does God allow hunger in the world?" Even when we

---

57   In the moment he said yes, but I'm prettttty sure he was sorry he asked.

don't know the answers, we've still got to be the place our kids come to for real answers from a Biblical perspective. That may mean we need to say, "I don't know, but let's research it together." An answer like this isn't *not* answering questions, rather it's caring enough to make sure you get the answer right. And you've still proven to be a safe place for your children where they know every question is okay and no topic is off limits.

BE THERE IN TRAGEDY

We all wish we could shield our children from death, loss, and crises. Tragedies in life are difficult for anyone, but when children go through their first experiences with true heartbreak it can be particularly devastating. When a great loss occurs, many parents believe their job is to be the strength of the family; to put on a happy face, and resist showing any emotion. According to this logic, the parent's composure in the face of tragedy helps everyone else believe they can overcome their personal pain and begin to heal. In most cases I'm afraid it doesn't quite work that way.

When we conceal our pain and sadness from our children we actually teach them it's not okay to be sad. They learn from us to push down their emotions and hide their true feelings. This does the opposite of promoting healing, it actually delays it and teaches harmful grieving practices. Parents who are emotionally available to their children in crises share their pain and sadness. They cry with their children. They look to the scriptures with their family for peace and rest. They demonstrate what it looks like to grieve with hope.

To be the parent for a child dealing with grief it's important to use simple and concrete language, let the child feel whatever he needs to feel, and speak truth without blaming God.[58] Let's break down each of those action steps for further explanation:

1. **Use simple and concrete language**—A lot of times we use euphemisms with children in order to "take the sting" out of tragic news. We'll say something like, "Grandma has gone to sleep," or, "Dad will now live in another house." Phrases like this are very confusing to children with no ability to think outside of concrete, black-and-white terms. As difficult as it is, it's best to speak plainly and get to the point. It may feel harsh, but

---

58   Two very old articles from Children's Ministry magazine have helped me learn a great deal about walking with kids through tragedies and death. They are Helping Children Deal With Death by Victor Parachin (July/August 1995) and Helping Children Grieve by Anthony M. Sirianni (January/February 1998). As of this writing, you can still find Parachin's piece on childrensministry.com.

the only way to help kids understand what they need to understand is to just say it.

2. **Let the child feel and act however they need**—Sometimes children want to play when everyone else wants to sit and talk. At times they laugh when the adults around them are crying. Their behavior can feel inappropriate and out of place, and often parents feel they should correct them and remind them of the gravity of the situation. Just as it's important to give children freedom to feel sad and cry, it's equally important to extend to them permission to feel happy or silly without guilt. I tell kids in crisis, "It's okay to feel however you want to feel. If you want to go outside and play basketball, that's fine. I'll play with you. If you want to sit and be quiet, we can do that too. If you want to cry or laugh… whatever, just know I'm here to listen when you're ready to talk." Make no mistake, children must go through the stages of grief just like adults, but due to their age and level of maturity it's going to look a lot different. And that's okay.

This advice may be a bit difficult for parents who are dealing with the effects of the crisis themselves. It can be difficult to help a child understand an emotional loss when you are coming to grips with the loss yourself. In these situations, it's a good idea to enlist the help of a pastor or trusted friend to walk alongside your child until you are emotionally available. That person can make sure the child is feeling what she needs to feel and working through pain. Still, you don't remove yourself from interaction with your child… She needs you, and it's still a good thing to show honest emotion. Rather, you explain that mom/dad is hurting too, and we all need people to help and support us.

3. **Speak truth without blaming God**—It is absolutely true that God is never caught off guard. I believe wholeheartedly that He has a perfect plan and nothing happens outside of His good and righteous will. That being said, sometimes we say things to hurting people that sound good, but actually cast blame on God, the Author of All Good Things, for the pain they are going through. Here are some examples of improper statements:

"This is God's will."

"God takes His favorites first. That's why your little sister is in Heaven now."

"Try to remember that God knew this divorce would happen and will use it for good."

Look, don't beat yourself up if you've said something like this to someone before. It's really tough to know what to say to hurting people. But think with me for just a moment what statements like this communicate to a kid. You've tried so hard to teach your child that God is a loving Father who wants the best for His children, yet now when He is needed the most He is painted as the source of their loss. How can God be a comfort when He is the one causing the pain? How can He be a Good Father when He makes His children feel this bad?

There are four simple truths I've learned to tell children in tragedy: "I don't know why this happened," "God loves," "God helps," and "God hears your prayers." Really, what we say doesn't matter nearly as much as our presence, engagement, kindness, and our listening ear. Still we want to represent God in the right way when we get the chance to speak truth into young, hurting hearts.

A great place to start with kids is to admit, "I don't know why this happened. I'm so sorry." Why is it so hard to say these words? We adults try so hard to take the tragedies of life and wrap them up with nice little bows for our children. We feel we have to always have an answer, so we use meaningless clichés and pretend we understand things we really don't. It's much better just to admit our limitation here and offer empathy. God *allows* certain bad things to happen, He never *causes* them, and we have no business claiming that we know His purposes that are so much higher than our comprehension. Even if we could, it wouldn't help the immediate grief of the child anyway.

Once I'm established in a situation as an empathetic listener, I want to reassure the child that God loves her, He will help her, and He listens to every single prayer… sad prayers, mad prayers, confused prayers… all of them. These three simple messages may sound trite, but they all point children back to seeking God for comfort and healing, rather than blaming Him for pain. I love to show children Psalm 34:18[59] and tell them, "God knows your heart is broken. He loves you and He makes things better. Maybe it doesn't seem like that right now, and that's okay. The Bible says He is near to you and He loves you so much."

---

59   The Lord is near the brokenhearted; He saves those crushed in spirit.-HCSB

Life comes with pain. We'd like to protect children from things that break their hearts, but if we did they'd never learn to love or trust or take risks. People will die, relationships will break down, things will be lost, and endeavors will fail. When they do, we've got to be the parent for young hearts that need help navigating grief.

So far we've talked about difficult ways parents must rise up and assume leadership roles. Sometimes though it's not difficult to do the things we're supposed to do. At times, being the parent means taking your daughter out for ice cream after a lousy day at school. It can mean teaching your son how to cast a fishing rod or scramble an egg for breakfast. Every day there are opportunities to rise up and fill our role as head of the house.

Are you ready to accept the mantra too? Only you can do it.

Be the parent.

Chapter Wrap Up

- We are not peers of our children. It is vital we rise to our God-ordained position in the home and not give away our parental authority. Be the parent!

- Children want and need defined limits from their parents. Boundaries give kids a sense of happiness and freedom in homes with safe and secure atmospheres.

- An important role for every parent is to answer every question using straightforward language without embarrassment. The moment we deflect or dodge a question from our kids, we cease to be a safe place for Godly counsel.

- Children dealing with grief need parents to use simple and concrete language, give permission to feel emotions freely, and speak truth without blaming God for the source of the pain.

Talk About It

The following are questions to answer yourself or talk about in a group.

1. After reading this chapter, what does the phrase "be the parent" mean to you?

2. What boundaries have you set up in your family to keep your children safe? What boundaries do you need to set up for continued vigilance?

3. What conversations are you tempted to avoid with your kids? What conversations do you need to have soon?

4. Have your children experienced crisis in their lives? If so, what did you learn about their grief? If not, how can you prepare now to help them in difficult times?

5. What are some instances not mentioned in this chapter in which you must "be the parent?" What can only you provide for them?

FROM GENERATION TO GENERATION

Noah and Lot.

Two men called "righteous" in the book of Genesis.

Both surrounded by immorality and godlessness, yet saved through miraculous, divine intervention.

One man's family repopulates the earth and gives rise to the people of God. The other's descendants become idol-worshiping enemies of the nation of Israel.

Two men, parallel stories, drastically different legacies.

Why?

Let me tell you a little more about Lot's story, and I think you'll see what led to such different outcomes. We'll begin with a seemingly simple choice Lot made, recorded in Genesis 13. Up until that time he lived with his uncle Abraham. Their combined households had grown very large and together they accumulated a vast wealth of livestock and resources. In fact, the family was so big that the land couldn't support them all anymore. Abraham knew they needed to split up, and although he was the elder in the clan and could choose for himself wherever he wanted to live, he humbly allowed Lot to choose the best land for his family and his animals to live. Lot went east and pitched his tents "near Sodom."[60] His uncle went the opposite direction.

Sodom was a bad place. It was full of wicked, depraved people who did wicked and depraved things. In fact, we find out in Genesis 18 that Sodom is so evil that God is ready to wipe the place completely from existence. He sends two angels to the town to carry out its destruction, and guess who they find living inside this godless town… Lot. He is no longer camped outside the town, he lives right in the middle of the immorality. Don't forget, Lot chose this. It was his decision to surround his family with the filth of unrighteousness.

Upon meeting, the angels tell Lot their plan to sleep in the town square that night, out in the open. Lot immediately knows this is an awful, terrible, dangerous idea. The people of Sodom were deplorable and treacherous… two strangers sleeping unprotected in public were extremely vulnerable to be victimized. Lot begged and pleaded for the angels to come to his home instead. Finally, they relented and agreed to stay with him.

But the night was far from over.

Later that evening the men of Sodom surrounded Lot's house. They yelled for Lot to send the two angels out of the house so they could have sex with them. Now Lot was in a tough predicament here, and rightfully he tried very hard to protect the angels under his care from this despicable act, but the solution he offered the crowd for appeasement was absolutely shocking:

> Lot went out to them at the entrance and shut the door behind him. He said, "Don't do this evil, my brothers. Look, I've got two daughters who haven't had sexual relations with a man. I'll bring them out to you, and you can do whatever you want to them. However, don't do anything to these men, because they have come under the protection of my roof." – Genesis 19:6-8 HCSB

Don't talk to me about historical context or cultural differences. Lot offered his own daughters to the disgusting mob. This is vile in every way. These two girls were "under his roof" just like the angels, but were not afforded the same protection. It's hard to argue that Lot had much value for his family legacy

---

60   Genesis 13:12

after this episode, and soon it would come back to haunt him.

The crowd turned down the offer of the girls and insisted on having their way with the new strangers in town, but at this point the angels had seen enough. God sent them to destroy Sodom and it was time to get down to business. First they struck the men closest to the house down to the ground with a blinding light. Then they said to Lot,

> *"Do you have anyone else here: a son-in-law, your sons and daughters, or anyone else in the city who belongs to you? Get them out of this place, for we are about to destroy this place because the outcry against its people is so great before the Lord, that the Lord sent us to destroy it."* – Genesis 19:12-13 HCSB

Here the comparison between Noah and Lot breaks down. God told Noah to do something crazy to save him and his family, he obeyed immediately, his family went along with the plan, and they were all miraculously saved. Obviously he had some credibility among his own household. Lot? Not so much. When the angels told him to gather his family, he went to his future sons-in-law to convince them to leave town. [61] They thought he was joking and laughed at him. Instead of allowing Lot to lead them to safety, they ignored his counsel and stayed in Sodom. When the city was destroyed, they died because Lot's word had no credibility in their lives.

And here's another example of Lot's poor family leadership— the next morning the angels had to urge Lot to leave *AGAIN!* If angels told me to leave because they were about to destroy my town, all you would see from me is taillights. Lot, his wife, and his two daughters went to bed and waited until the next morning to leave. At that point the angels hurried them outside the city and told them to run away from Sodom, don't stop, don't even look back. They eventually got out of town, but because Lot dragged his feet, his wife was close enough when the destruction occurred to disobey the angels' order and turn back to watch. Instantly she turned into a pillar of salt. Unlike Noah, Lot didn't obey God's directive immediately and his family paid dearly for the delay.

Two sons-in-law dead. Wife dead. Two daughters devastated and let down by the man who was supposed to protect them. This is the legacy this family patriarch left behind. Soon those girls would pay him back for his sin and do

---

61   The guys who were supposed to marry the girls who Lot offered up earlier. Where were they when that was going down, by the way. Sounds like a couple of winning fiancées.

something equally despicable, resulting in generations of people at war with the people of God.[62]

But wait, you say. I thought Moses, the writer of Genesis, called Lot a "righteous man?" Can a righteous man leave such a lousy legacy behind? The answer is apparently, yes. King Josiah's great grandfather is another example.

KING JOSIAH'S GREAT GRANDFATHER

The story of King Josiah from 2 Kings 22 is a great one to share with children. He became King of Judah at the young age of 8 and led the people with Godly wisdom for 31 years. After ruling for about 18 years, Josiah began a project to restore the temple of God which had been neglected and abused for decades. During the temple renovation a forgotten book of holy scriptures was discovered. When King Josiah read the long lost laws of God, it caused him great anguish. He immediately recognized his people were not living according to the scriptures, so he called the entire nation together to repent and recommit to following the law. His godly leadership resulted in revival across Judah. It's a great story to help children understand that even young people can make good choices and do important things for God.

But it leads to a couple of obvious questions: Why was the temple such a mess and why had the Word of God been abandoned and forgotten by the people of Judah? Josiah's father Amon was part of the problem. He was a wicked king who worshiped idols, did evil in the sight of the Lord, and led people away from God. He only served two years before being killed by his own servants.

Josiah's grandfather Manasseh was even worse. He worshiped foreign gods, set up idols in the holy temples, and performed "detestable practices" before God. In 2 Kings 21 we discover that, "...he shed so much innocent blood that he filled Jerusalem with it from one end to another."[63] Worse, he led Israelites living in Judah away from following the One True God. The entire country suffered under his rule.

But what about Manasseh's father? Who was he to leave behind such a lousy legacy? Surprisingly, he was a great man of God named Hezekiah. Here is how he is described in 2 Kings 18:5-6:

---

62   You can find more on the conclusion of this story in Genesis 19.
63   HCSB

Hezekiah trusted in the Lord God of Israel; not one of the kings of Judah was like him, either before him or after him. He remained faithful to Yahweh and did not turn from following Him but kept the commands the Lord had commanded Moses.[64]

Hezekiah was a great man of God who faced incredible challenges in his time with faith and devotion. Things were tough during his reign... Judah experienced constant threat from the Assyrian Empire. Through it all Hezekiah sought the Lord and remained reliant on God's power. How could such a faithful man raise a son and grandson bent toward so much evil? A seemingly insignificant event toward the end of his life gives us a small clue. Here's what happened:

Toward the end of Hezekiah's life he received some visitors from Babylon, a colony of the Assyrian kingdom. He proudly showed off his wealth to his guests by giving them a tour of the entire palace. He even took them into his armory and treasure room to show them the *good stuff*- silver, gold, spices, precious oils, etc. This was a pretty dumb way for Hezekiah to stroke his own ego. Showing a neighboring country with a vested interest in conquering your land all your riches is a great way to give them even more motivation. When his contemporary, the prophet Isaiah, found out that the visitors had seen everything, he told Hezekiah that because of his pride one day the Babylonians would come back and steal all the wealth they had seen, and even take some of the people of Judah as captives. Hezekiah's response is somewhat surprising,

Then Hezekiah said to Isaiah, "The word of the Lord you have spoken is good, for he thought: Why not, if there will be peace and security during my lifetime?" – 2 Kings 20:19 HCSB

Did you catch that? The entire nation of Judah would suffer for Hezekiah's sin of pride, but he was cool with it because the punishment would come after his death. He was fine with poverty and captivity for his own people... no problem. It wouldn't affect his present reality. Let his ancestors deal with it. No wonder his own son overturned every good thing he'd ever done as king. Hezekiah had no interest in leaving a legacy or worrying about future generations, and his family and his kingdom crumbled the moment he breathed his last breath.

---

64   HCSB

The answer is yes. You can follow God without intentionally letting your faith flow down to your children and your children's children. There is more evidence in the Bible still:

- Eli the priest and mentor to Samuel neglected to raise his sons well and allowed them to use their position in the temple to gain sex and wealth.[65]

- Speaking of Samuel, his sons Joel and Abijah were known for taking bribes, doing dishonest deals, and perverting justice. They were supposed to follow in Samuel's footsteps and become judges over the people, but due to immorality were deemed unfit for the position. Their failure disqualified them from leading and led the people of Israel to completely reject the rule of judges over the country. Instead of anointing his children, Samuel was soon anointing Saul and David as the first kings of Israel. [66]

- And since we brought up King David, we might as well climb out on his family tree too. Did you realize that all of his first six sons were born to different mothers? Some of his children displayed terrible behavior, yet David rarely did anything to correct, admonish, or parent them in any way. One of his sons named Amnon raped his half-sister Tamar. Another son Absolum killed Amnon for his actions and eventually raised up an army in an unsuccessful attempt to overthrow David as king.[67]

"The only thing that matters in the end is that God's kingdom advances and His name is glorified."

The list goes on and on. The Bible is full of examples of parents who didn't lead their children in the faith. But even though some of these people were still considered "righteous" by God, they always paid a great price for not investing in future generations. Look at the pain, loss, and devastation in just the stories I've shared in this chapter... the ramifications of these bad dads' actions (or inactions) affected millions of people across several generations. Clearly their failure had significant negative impact on the Kingdom of God.

Of course we want more than that for those who come behind us!

65   1 Samuel 2
66   1 Samuel 8
67   1 Samuel 13-18

Our children are the ones who must carry on the work of the gospel to the world. Faith can't stop with us; it must flow down. I love the imagery the Psalmist uses in Psalm 127 concerning the impact children can make in the world:

Like arrows in the hand of a warrior are the sons born in one's youth. – Psalm 127:4 HCSB

An arrow in the hand of a skilled warrior can travel farther and do more damage in battle than the warrior ever could on his own. The same is true for our children. Whether we like it or not, they will leave our house one day. They will go places we will never go and meet people we will never meet. On that day our names and our reputations won't mean anything. The things we've bought and provided for them will be rusted, broken, and decayed. The inheritance we've worked so hard to leave behind will be spent. Our accomplishments wiped from memory. The only thing... the *ONLY THING* that matters in the end is that God's kingdom advances and His Name is glorified. Our faith is really the only lasting legacy we have to pass down.

My grandfather is a spiritual giant in my life. His name was Dr. James L. Monroe (the grandkids called him Poppy) and he was a pastor for over 60 years. In fact, he led the church I grew up in as a child and remains vivid in my memory as a great man of God. I'm not the only one who thought of him that way... he was beloved by so many in that church who looked to him as counselor, shepherd, and mentor. When he retired from the pulpit he turned his efforts to mission work around the world. After years of working with several countries through what was then called The Foreign Mission Board, he focused his work on the country of Indonesia. There he helped local believers build a church, found a university, and carry the gospel to people living in areas hostile to Christianity. While in college I got to go with him to the country he loved and see him in action among the church people and college students hungry for Christ. I was sixty years younger but I could barely keep up.

Honestly I didn't know how far reaching Poppy's influence was until he died. Respect and well-wishes poured in from around the world. I learned that he was a "pastor's pastor" from a number of ministers who shared about the many times he'd helped them through difficult times or provided Godly wisdom that changed them for the better. Missionaries, international ministry leaders, business leaders, and even a senator honored my grandfather with testimonials about his impact during his memorial service. When Billy and Ruth Graham found out he died, they wrote a letter to my grandmother saying, "We praise God for the life of this godly man, and are thankful for the privilege of knowing him." I wish you could have known him too.

Poppy's father, my great grandfather was also a man of faith. His name was Claude Lester Monroe and he was a fireman. He absolutely loved everything having to do with firefighting and would talk about it with anyone who would listen. He was a big guy… a gentle giant who was kind, loving, and strong. He is remembered as a great man.

But not by me.

My great grandfather died in 1974, three years before I was born. I'm sorry to say I didn't even know his name until I asked my mom about him for this chapter.[68] I'm sure someone in my family told me stories about him as a child, but we don't talk about him anymore. Long ago he slipped from my memory.

I didn't know Claude Lester Monroe, but I know his faith. His faith flowed down to my grandfather, then down to my mom, and then down to me. Ultimately that's what matters most. Now it's my job to keep the legacy going to the next generation.

And it's your job in your home.

STARTING A NEW LEGACY

Maybe you're like Josiah. Maybe your parents and your parents' parents were not people of faith. Or maybe they were, but had no value for passing their faith down. No one modeled for you in your home what it meant to follow Jesus and now you feel a bit like a sailor without a compass, trying to sail through the waters of family discipleship without a clue where you're heading. First I must tell you, I'm so proud of you. When you picked up this book, you proved you care about passing down faith to your kids, and that alone matters a lot. And now through reading you've learned it might not be as difficult as you thought: love God, let His Word fill you up, let it overflow into your family. If I've tried to communicate anything to you at this point, it's this: **YOU CAN DO THIS!** Through God's help you can lead your family through seized, created, and special opportunities.

I also want to tell you you're not alone. A lot of us in this generation are hav-

---

68   Hey mom.

ing to reorient our values and behaviors to figure out spiritual leadership. Let me tell you why: Two big events in our nation's recent history have changed family dynamics dramatically: the industrial revolution in the 1800s and the sexual revolution of the 60s and 70s. The sexual revolution brought about new ideas about the purpose of marriage, roles within marriage, the definition of marriage and family, and significantly delayed the average ages for marriage and the birth of a couple's first child. These changing values and beliefs were followed swiftly by the divorce boom of the eighties. Our country is still feeling the effects of these shifts today.

Believe it or not, the industrial revolution might have been an even bigger shift for families living in America. Before the 19th century most families lived together on farms. The home was the center of economic, social, spiritual, and educational life. Extended families lived together, supporting one another and depending on one another for survival... everyone pitched in to provide the necessities of life. The more children in your home, the more people you had working in the field, so kids were considered assets for economic growth. And then the industrial revolution happened. For the first time men, women, and even children left the home to make money, usually in a factory. No longer were families working together for mutual benefit, the only connection they had was pooled resources and limited time together. Kids shifted from assets to liabilities in the family makeup— more mouths to feed— so parents started having less children. Services sprung up to take the place of things that used to happen in the home: schooling, rec leagues, fast food restaurants, and yes... Christian education. When the home stopped being the center of family life the era of outsourcing began.[69]

This is the culture our parents were born into. They are first or second generation results of moms and dads leaving the home to find work elsewhere. They were the guinea pigs of outsourced parenting. As a result, many of them didn't have spiritual discipleship modeled for them either. They thought they were doing well enough by dropping kids off at Sunday School once or twice a week for the "experts" to give them a lesson and a flower-shaped butter cookie. Now we know better.

I'm praying for this generation of parents to diverge from the previous generations. Those that came before us weren't bad people, they did the best with what they had. We know now that relying on a church program to raise

---

69   Diana R. Garland, Family Ministry: A Comprehensive Guide (Downers Grove, Illinois: IVP Academic, 2012), 32-40.

up spiritual champions isn't the most effective plan. Sure, many of us are still leaving the home to earn income, but we know spiritual growth is something we just can't outsource to someone else. Our homes must be the place our kids grow to become disciples of Christ. Or on busy days, the car or the fast food booth. Now it's time for us to take the baton and run on for the sake of our children. We do that by intentionally investing in their spiritual growth every single day.

So now it's time to break some old generational cycles. The absence of spiritual conversation between family members can be reversed. The "drop your kids off at church and hope for the best" mindset can stop today with you. You can create new traditions, new values, and new practices right now that can be repeated by your children. Then hopefully one day by your children's children. You didn't have a road map for home discipleship, but that doesn't mean you can't leave one behind for future generations.

SUMMARY
Let's take a moment before we wrap things up to review what we've covered in the last eight chapters. Go slowly through these points… These are our major takeaways:

- You are the most important spiritual leader in your child's life.

- The **Shema** found in **Deuteronomy 6** tells us the two most important things a parent can do to develop faith in a child is to **love God yourself** with heart, soul, and strength; then **let God's Word overflow** into teaching opportunities with kids.

- Spiritual leadership doesn't have to be an unrealistic, unattainable model that leaves you feeling ill-equipped and utterly defeated as the leader of your home. You can **seize opportunities**, **create opportunities**, and take advantage of **special opportunities** to speak God's truth into your family. **You really can do this**.

- **Children are different from adults**. Their stage of development, cultural complexity, and individuality means that we have to be students of our kids and refrain from turning our own history, limitations, and preferences into expectations for them.

- As you lead your home, at some point your child must answer God's call and choose for himself to follow Jesus. You gauge his readiness for a life of faith two ways: **relying on the Holy Spirit's guidance** and watching for **personal awareness of their great need for Jesus**.

- When guiding children into a life of faith, it's important to use **active language** that calls them to actively respond to the gospel, rather than **passive language** that merely suggests they "agree" with some teachings in scripture. Jesus is interested in more than a prayer, He desires surrender and life change even for kids.

- Although their young brains understand the world differently, kids can absolutely choose salvation through Jesus for themselves. What kids need to know about the gospel can be categorized into five topics: **God's love, sin and consequence, Jesus is the only answer, it's your choice,** and **the free gift**.

- A family of faith should be different from other families in the world. We must make choices that honor God regardless of what others do around us. A good place to start living a countercultural life of faith is to **talk** about decision-making at home, **commit to your local church**, and capture opportunities to **serve** together.

- No one else can instill the discipline our children need. No one can set up appropriate boundaries to keep our children from harm, answer questions accurately and honestly from a biblical perspective, and walk with our children through tragedy like mom or dad. That's why we must rise up and **be the parent.**

- Biblically, it's possible to be considered "righteous" and still have no value for letting faith flow down. However, that lack of value always comes with a cost, usually paid by the generations to come. We want more for our children and our grandchildren. We want to pass along a **legacy of faith** by the way we value and lead our families today.

So, you've learned all this. Now what? Each of us, regardless of our parenting stage has a next step we can take today toward better leadership in the home. Maybe you need to be more intentional and find opportunities to speak biblical truth to your kids. Maybe you need to identify the spirit of defeat that has crippled your spiritual leadership long enough and cast it down through the power of God's grace. Maybe it's time to add scripture memory or highlighter talks to your daily schedule. Maybe it's time for your family to go on a mission trip. Whatever it is, here's my advice: identify your next step and take it. Don't take eight next steps. Just take one.

Then, when God calls you to take another step, take that one.

This isn't a race and it surely isn't a list to check off. No matter what any expert says, there is no sure-fire recipe for perfect children in 10 days. Family leadership is a marathon, not a sprint. You never see the same Olympians compete in the 100-meter sprint and the 10,000-meter long distant event. You know why? The sprinters are built for short bursts of speed. Sure, they run much faster than the long distance guys and girls, but they can't sustain their speed for more than a few seconds.

The long distance runners are in it for the long haul. They'll set a pace in the beginning and gradually build speed until they reach the finish line. This is the example for us... we want to continually take next steps that teach and model faith in our homes until we launch our kids into the world ready to live by faith. This is how real, lasting legacies are made.

So, what's your next step? What do you need to do starting today to build your legacy of faith? It might be a good idea to stop reading for a moment and prayerfully consider the work God wants to do in you to move you forward as a spiritual leader. I'll even give you a spot right here if you want to write your next step of faith:

MY NEXT STEP

_____

_____

_____

_____

_____

_____

_____

_____

_____

_____

You've made it to the end of the book, and we've covered a lot of ground. Now all that's left is to put faith in action in your family. Every faith talk, every seized opportunity, every teachable moment could have ramifications that span across the generations. You can do this. It matters. Your family is your most important ministry.

FAITH

FLOWS

DOWN.

You are exactly the one God intended to show kids what it means to be a disciple. No one else has the time, the prominence, or the platform that you do with your children. Your job is to draw close to God and then let what He starts in you flow over into your family. It's time to start now. You're ready.

So breathe in. Breathe out.

Love God.

Lead your home.

Chapter Wrap Up

- It is possible to be righteous, yet have no value for letting faith flow down to future generations. However, to build a lasting legacy of faith we must invest now in our children.

- For some, the call of God is to continue a legacy of faith started long ago. Others must work to start a brand new tradition of spiritual leadership.

- Even in families of faith, spiritual leadership was not modeled for many in previous generations. Old cycles of neglect and outsourcing must be broken for homes to become the center of faith development.

- Every reader of this book has a next step to take toward becoming the spiritual leader of the family. Pray today for God to reveal it to you and help you lead your family for the glory of God.

Talk About It

The following are questions to answer yourself or talk about in a group.

1. How has *Faith Flows Down* inspired you to better lead your home spiritually?

2. What is one change you will make immediately in your home?

3. What are your dreams for future generations?

4. What is the spiritual legacy of your family? Do you need to continue the faith of those who came before or start a new legacy?

5. What will you do now to make those dreams a reality?

Know that Yahweh your God is God, the faithful God who keeps His gracious covenant loyalty for a thousand generations with those who love Him and keep His commands.

Deuteronomy 7:9 HCSB

Appendix One:
Highlighter Talks

Highlighter Talks are a quick, simple way for you and your child to talk about God's Word every single day. You don't have to gather any supplies, prepare any lessons, or even study ahead of time. You and your child will simply open the Bible and interact with the truth you find. It is a very casual, informal way for you to begin filling your child's heart with God's Word, create opportunities for spiritual conversation, and help your child develop a resource for life.

What your child will need: A Bible, Five Highlighters: yellow, pink, green, blue, orange

What you will need: The *Highlighter Talks* scripture list at the end of this section

How to conduct Highlighter Talks:

1. Select a scripture from the Highlighter Talks scripture list to discuss with your child. The scriptures are broken into five different categories that can be done in any order you choose. You may also add any scriptures to the list that you want to introduce to your child.

2. Ask your child to find the scripture and read it out loud.

3. Ask your child, "What do you think this verse means?" Remember during this time that there are no wrong answers. Allow your child to interact simply and purely with God's Word.

4. Tell your child what the verse means to you. This isn't to correct your child's understanding or clarify the truth (although that often will occur). You do this so your child can hear you interact with scripture too and watch you value the truth in the Bible.

5. Ask your child to highlight the verse using the correct category color.

And that's it! It is so simple and easy, but you are doing several things that will make an impact eternally in your child's life:

You are helping your child develop a habit of daily Bible reading.

You are leading spiritually in your home.

Your child is creating a resource to find important scriptures in his or her own Bible.

Your child is learning and discussing valuable truth.

Don't worry about how much you know or how well you can teach the Bible. Just have a conversation with your child beginning with a simple verse. Anyone can do it.

Helpful Hints:

- Take some days off from your list to go on "Highlighter Hunts." Challenge your child to flip through his or her Bible to find a verse that has been previously marked. Once a verse has been found, have him or her read and discuss the scripture again. This will help you review past readings, as well as make it fun for your child.

- Stay consistent, but don't worry if you miss a day. The nature of Highlighter Talks allows you to pick up right where you left off. Don't let discouragement keep you from being the leader God called you to be in your home.

Highlighter Talks Scripture List:

Yellow: God's Value for You
1. John 3:16
2. Jeremiah 29:11
3. 1 John 3:1
4. Romans 8:28
5. Ephesians 2:4-5
6. 1 Peter 5:7
7. 1 John 4:10
8. Psalm 23:6
9. Luke 12:6–7
10. Psalm 139:14

Green: Living God's Way

1. Ephesians 6:10-11
2. Galatians 2:20
3. Philippians 4:4-8
4. 1 Peter 5:6-7
5. Matthew 22:37-40
6. 1 Peter 4:7-8
7. Proverbs 3:5-6
8. Colossians 3:2
9. Psalm 139:23-24
10. Galatians 5:22-23
11. Acts 20:35
12. Matthew 5:14-16
13. 1 Corinthians 13:4-7
14. Hebrews 11:6
15. Philippians 2:14-15
16. Romans 12:2
17. Micah 6:8
18. Matthew 16:33

Orange: Talking with God

1. Jeremiah 33:3
2. Matthew 6:9-13
3. John 15:7
4. James 5:6
5. 1 Timothy 2:8
6. Matthew 18:20
7. 1 Thessalonians 5:16-18
8. 1 John 5:14
9. Colossians 4:2
10. Psalm 145:18

Blue: The Bible's Importance

1. Psalm 119:9-11
2. Psalm 119:105
3. Hebrews 4:12
4. Psalm 40:8
5. 2 Timothy 3:16
6. Isaiah 40:8
7. Matthew 24:35

8. James 1:22
9. Matthew 7:24
10. Luke 11:28

Pink: Jesus' Work in our Lives
1. John 10:10
2. Philippians 4:13
3. Acts 2:38
4. Psalm 27:1
5. Romans 3:23
6. Romans 6:23
7. Romans 5:8
8. Romans 10:9
9. Luke 19:10
10. John 15:5
11. John 14:6
12. John 3:3
13. Matthew 10:32
14. 2 Corinthians 5:17
15. 1 John 1:9

Appendix Two:
Art Murphy's Five Questions
from "The Faith of a Child"

There is simply too much wisdom in these five questions for me not to include them in this book. They are extremely helpful when trying to evaluate your child's readiness to make the choice to follow Christ. All the information below is pulled from "Chapter Five: How to Know if a Child is Ready to Become a Christian" from the book *The Faith of a Child* by Art Murphy.[70]

1. Does salvation make sense?
Can your child repeat the Gospel back to you? Has he connected Jesus' death on the cross and resurrection with his own personal need? Has he grasped the basics of following Jesus? Can he tell you the difference between salvation and baptism?

2. Does the child exhibit a brokenness over sin?
Does your child know he is a sinner? Can he connect the consequences of his sin with his spiritual reality? Does he know why he needs Jesus? Is salvation merely a "good idea" or an urgency on his heart?

3. Is the child serious about this commitment?
Does he approach the gospel flippantly? Is his decision to follow Christ more important to him or you? Does he bring up the subject of becoming a Christian or do you have to push the conversation?

4. Is the child's decision self-made?
Is this choice a way of getting public praise or pleasing his family or peer group? Does your child feel left out because his friends have recently made a decision to
follow Christ or get baptized? Do you suspect he's being influenced to make the decision by something other than the call of the Father?

5. Has the child's decision been sealed?
Has he "officially" prayed or committed to surrender his life to Christ. Was there a moment of decision in which the child acknowledged his need for

---

70   Art Murphy, The Faith of a Child (Chicago, Illinois: Moody, 2000).

Christ and expressed the choice to repent, follow, and trust Jesus? Was this event marked as the day of salvation or spiritual birthday of the child?

Appendix Three:
The ABCs of Salvation

For many, many years children's ministers have used the letters *A*, *B*, and *C* to help children understand how to surrender their lives to Jesus. This is a simple strategy and by no means exhaustive concerning the teachings of scripture on salvation, but it does break this all-important decision down into three components that children can easily understand. Often, kids are ready to make a decision for Christ, but don't have words to convey the commitment they feel they need to make. The ABCs give words to deep convictions in their hearts. Now, remember this truth from chapter five: mere words spoken out loud do not replace a genuine decision for life change. There is nothing magical about the words represented by the letters A, B, and C. Use this tool only as a guide to help children surrender to God's call once they understand the depth of commitment required.

A- Admit

A child must admit before God that he is a sinner in need of forgiveness. Really this goes back to acknowledging our need for a Savior. Unless you understand your sin, you really can't understand why you need saving. In order for children to surrender to a life of faith, they must come in humility before God and confess those things that have severed the holy relationship they were meant to experience in the Father's presence. This is the right posture required to follow Jesus and receive His free gift.

B- Believe

Children must declare they believe that Jesus is God's Son, He died on the cross, rose again, is alive forevermore, and accepts all who choose to follow Him. This active response word comes from Paul's words recorded in Romans 10:9:

> *If you confess with your mouth, "Jesus is Lord," and believe in your heart that God raised Him from the dead, you will be saved.*[71]

I say belief is an active response, because true belief requires action. If you truly believe, you will confess "Jesus is Lord" to the people who you come in contact with on a daily basis. If you truly believe you will alter

_____
71   HCSB

135

your decision-making process to accommodate the object of your faith.

A common way to teach active belief to children is to reference a chair. You can ask a child, "Do you believe that if you sit on this chair it will hold you up?" When the child answers, "yes," you can then ask, "how would you prove that you believe in that chair?" Of course, the child will then plop himself down on the chair. He has just demonstrated active belief. You can explain to him that just like he showed his belief in the chair by sitting down, he must show his belief in Jesus by placing his life completely in God's hands. That means showing His belief in God's Word by making choices which line up with teachings in scripture. That means living by faith and trusting that God hears and answers every prayer. It's not enough to just say we believe in God, our belief must take action.

In the same way faith, if it doesn't have works, is dead by itself.[72]

C- Choose

There's actually a couple of C's floating around out there promoted by different ministries. Some would say the C stands for the word *confess,* others might use *commit.* Both of those terms are Biblically sound and appropriate when sharing the Gospel, but when kids are ready to follow Jesus themselves, I prefer to coach them to *choose* following Jesus.

Choosing is an active response concept that helps kids know they are responsible for making the decision to follow Jesus. At the moment of salvation they should declare before God that Jesus alone will be the King of their life, and nothing else will rise above Him for first place.

It's always a good idea when speaking to a child about choice to remind them about repentance. Remember, repentance is the choice to **stop** going the wrong direction (making choices that don't honor God, following selfish desires instead of God's best, etc.), **turn** your back on your old way of living, and **choose to go a new direction** (following Jesus).[73] When children are ready to surrender to Christ, repentance must be a part of the decision.

Using the ABCs at Home

When your child is ready to follow Jesus, it is appropriate for him to make the

---

72   James 2:17 HCSB
73   For more information on repentance go to chapter five.

decision with a prayer. Kids can express their choice with eyes open, eyes closed, sitting in a chair, standing on their head, alone, or with a parent... the how doesn't matter. What does matter is that there is a clear, identifiable moment when the choice was actually made. Likewise, the words of the prayer don't matter. It's all about the heart of the decision. But, if kids want help putting language to their commitment, you can explain the ABCs and then give them a sample prayer as a guide. A prayer using the ABC's typically goes like this:

Dear Jesus,
I **admit** that I am a sinner. I've done things, said things, and thought things that displeased you. Please forgive me of my sins. I **believe** in You. I believe you died for my sins and then rose again. I believe you are alive forever. I **choose** today to follow You. I want you to be King of my life. I promise to love You, trust You, and live how You want me to live. Thank You for saving me, Jesus.
Amen

There's absolutely nothing wrong with sharing this example with children and then encouraging them to use it to express the decision their hearts want to make. Where you can go wrong here is giving these words to a child who doesn't understand the gospel and then have him repeat it without full understanding. This tool is for when the moment of decision emerges. The ABCs simply put words to the commitment God calls children to make. Admit, believe, and choose... seize the moment of decision and help your child know these are the right responses to the gospel to begin a life of faith.

Find more resources for your family at
watershedfamilies.org

watershed
FAMILY RESOURCES